Refuse To Sink

Stories of Life, Loss, Love, and Laughter

By

Kelly Guay

This book is dedicated to my four amazing children. I love you more than chocolate.

Joni, Hanna, Brody, and Maddox

Table of Contents

Foreword	12
Introduction	19
Anchored	23
Greyson	26
Happy Birthday!	31
Summah Time	33
Thank You	37
Warriors	40
Widow Dating	44
Things I Want My Kids to Know	50

Moms I Don't Get	57
Let it Go	61
Mike	68
Yuletide Cheer	72
Mahalo	79
A Mom's Twelve Days of Christmas	82
Mom	88
Please Don't Feel Bad for Me	93
Comp Mom	98
Friends	102
Life Skills	106

Oxygen Mask	111
Cloned	115
Kels	123
An Open Letter to my Husband on the Anniversary of Your Passing	127
Road Trip Lessons with My Kids	134
Speeding Through Life	138
Small Town	142
Dad	151
I Love it When	157
Homesick	162

3 Years	169
Beach Days	175
Siblings	178
Is That a Donut?	181
42 and 1 to Grow	186
I Believe	198
Joan	202
Strength	207
What's Your Excuse?	211
4 Years Later…	217
Wooden Bats	223

For the Love of Food	234
Thanks Mom	239
We Do Messy	243
Love	249
Oh, The Places I've Been	259
10 Positive Things About the Quarantine	269
Together	271
Your Letter	278
It's Not Just a Car	287
My Big Brother	295

Happy Holidays	299
Afterword	316

Foreword

By

Daisy Mirzaei

"Hope is the anchor of the soul." No truer words have been written than this. When I first heard this phrase, I had no idea what it meant. When one hears the word "anchor", one usually thinks of the device, usually of metal, attached to a ship or boat by a cable or chain that is lowered to the seabed to hold the vessel in a particular place while in a body of water. To me, when I hear the word "anchor", I think of protection, security and safeguard. An anchor helps to keep us grounded and in one place when things are turbulent and unsettling around us. I am a mother to three children and my eldest was diagnosed with a serious medical condition early in life. If anyone needed an anchor, it was me. Let me introduce you to three of my most steadfast anchors.

My dad has always been a steady and resilient figure in my life. He was a very traditional, Chinese father and believed the key to a good life laid in having a solid education. My dad was born and raised in China and Hong Kong. He immigrated to the US when he was a teenager.

While he worked in his family's restaurants, he enlisted in the US Army and went to college to obtain his engineering degree. He taught my little brother and I how important family was and to never forget where we came from. To me, my father was larger than life and someone, to this day, I still aspire to be. He married the love of his life, my late mother, only to lose her to breast cancer in 1986. I remember how heartbroken he was over his loss but also how he picked himself up in order to raise my little brother and me. Everything that he promised my late mother, he did from ensuring my little brother and my education to keeping watch over my late mother's mother. In my father, I had an example of what strength, discipline and a never-ending love was.

With my husband, Saman, I always tell people, "He is everything that I am not. This is why our marriage works." During the first year of parenthood, maneuvering through our second year of marriage was very difficult. When Isabelle was first diagnosed with Cooley's Anemia, he 100% blamed me for everything that was happening to her. Since I already blamed myself, I took it until I could not anymore. I had my dad to thank for that. My dad saw how I constantly beat myself up and one day he said to me, "Daisy, you are no good to Belle Belle and Sam like this. In order to get through this, you have to be strong. I know you and this is not you." He was right. This was not me. What I was doing served no purpose to my little girl or my marriage. I also came to realize that my husband constantly blaming me served no purpose. Sam and I sat down one day and laid everything out on the table. Do we continue together or do we go our separate ways? At that time, we shared our feelings about what was going on for the first time and saw each other in a new light. We agreed to work on our marriage and raise our daughter together because we knew that where one lacked, the other made up for it. Sam is like the night. I am more like the day. Sam is quiet. I am very talkative. Sam likes quiet work and being a pharmacist suits him. I like hustle and bustle and interacting with people, so being a nurse suits me. We have been married now for 15 years and counting, with not only one, but three beautiful daughters. Our marriage is a strong one filled with laughter, yelling and tears, but mostly laughter. In my husband, my daughters have someone to compare their future spouses to. Through everything, the good, the bad and the ugly, Sam has remained constant and strong in his commitment to our family.

When my eldest daughter, Isabelle, was born, she was diagnosed with Cooley's Anemia. She was seen at the Tomorrow Fund Clinic at Hasbro Children's Hospital in Providence, Rhode
Island. During the early days, being scared witless pretty much summed up how I was feeling. Though Sam and I were both healthcare professionals, nothing prepared us for being parents to a child with a life-threatening medical diagnosis. On the surface, Isabelle was a beautiful little girl with jet black hair and the rosiest, fattest cheeks. She was such a good baby and Sam and I fell head over heels in love with her. On the inside, her

body started betraying her when she was six months old by not producing red blood cells they way it should have. By the time she was 11 months old, she would have her first blood transfusion and would continue these every three to four weeks for the next 11 years. The staff of the Tomorrow Fund Clinic take care of the most vulnerable patients, pediatric patients. Though it is difficult work, they never faltered in their job to care for the children who came under their care. It was Dr. Chawla and Jodi Lochotzki, RN who would help us more than we could have ever imagined. They were not only full of medical knowledge, but they were full of support, encouragement, kindness and love. They never made us feel like inept parents. Even after Isabelle went on to transplant at Boston Children's Hospital, they were still with us every step of the way. Now that I look back on our 11 years at the Tomorrow Fund Clinic, they were not just our medical team, but they became our family that helped lift us out of the dark.

While Izzy was still being seen at The Tomorrow Fund Clinic, I was able to meet other parents who also had children who had life threatening and being a pharmacist suits him. I like hustle and bustle and interacting with people, so being a nurse suits me. We have been married now for 15 years and counting, with not only one, but three beautiful daughters. Our marriage is a strong one filled with laughter, yelling and tears, but mostly laughter. In my husband, my daughters have someone to compare their future spouses to. Through everything, the good, the bad and the ugly, Sam has remained constant and strong in his commitment to our family.

When my eldest daughter, Isabelle, was born, she was diagnosed with Cooley's Anemia. She was seen at the Tomorrow Fund Clinic at Hasbro Children's Hospital in Providence, Rhode Island. During the early days, being scared witless pretty much summed up how I was feeling. Though Sam and I were both healthcare professionals, nothing prepared us for being parents to a child with a life-threatening medical diagnosis. On the surface, Isabelle was a beautiful little girl with jet black hair and the rosiest, fattest cheeks. She was such a good baby and Sam and I fell head over heels in love with her. On the inside, her body started betraying her when she was six months old by not producing red blood cells they way it should have. By the time she was 11 months old, she would have her first blood transfusion and would continue these every three to four weeks for the next 11 years. The staff of the Tomorrow Fund Clinic take care of the most vulnerable patients, pediatric patients. Though it is difficult work, they never faltered in their job to care for the children who came under their care. It was Dr. Chawla and Jodi Lochotzki, RN who would help us more than we could have ever imagined. They were not only full of medical knowledge, but they were full of support, encouragement, kindness and love. They never made us feel like inept parents. Even after Isabelle went on to transplant at Boston Children's Hospital, they were still with us every step of the way. Now that I look back on our 11 years at the Tomorrow Fund Clinic, they were not just our medical team, but they became our family that helped lift us out of the dark.

 While Izzy was still being seen at The Tomorrow Fund Clinic, I was able to meet other parents who also had children who had life threatening diagnoses/disorders. One of those moms who has constantly remained by my side is the author of this book. Her story is one of heartbreak, resilience, and triumph. It is because of Kelly that I first heard the term "Refuse to Sink". This is the name of her blog that she shared with me, as well as her unfailing support and friendship.

Kelly shared with me her remarkable life story and the amazingly strong and ever-present anchors in her life. Through everything she has gone through, she remains unsinkable and steady, much like an anchor. I invite you to read and get to know the amazing and wonderful woman I have come to know. I also invite you, as you read her story, to think about the anchors in your life. Kelly made me think of all the people who have become my anchors and I started to see and appreciate them more for the steadfast and loving parts they have played and continue to play in my life.

Introduction

My brother, David mark, died when he was 8 years old on the birthday he shared with my father. David had been sick for about 3 years, diagnosed with aplastic anemia. It is now a disease that offers treatments with extremely high success rates in children, unlike in the 1970's. My parents were in their early thirties and David was their 1st child. Despite my parent's loss and all they went through; I still had an amazing childhood. I remember my mother always smiling and positive. Her attitude was contagious. My dad was the same, always giving us a way to change our thinking to see the bright side of situations and the good side of people as well. Growing up in this atmosphere gave me a strong foundation for resiliency. I am forever grateful. The word resilient is defined by Webster's Dictionary as "an ability to recover from or adjust easily to misfortune or change". Throughout my life, I, like most others, have experienced much misfortune and change. My ability to recover and adjust has been a gift. I attribute it to my upbringing, but also as a true gift from God. I see so many others that cannot seem to see beyond their own misfortune. Instead of pushing through to recover, they are stuck. Many times, they are stuck in self-pity and too many times this leads to far worse problems than with what they began.

I remember all too clearly when my mom told me she had leukemia and even clearer the day she died, just three months later. What sticks out in my head is one thought that I had over and over again. If my mom and dad can go through the hell of losing a child and still raise their living children as positively and happily as we were raised, then I too could see the hope. I too could smile and would again. I could get through the pain, no matter what it took. None of it was easy. I searched for something, someone who could help. It didn't happen overnight, but I did heal. I made my mind up to heal. I still miss my mom. I always will. I miss all of my loved ones who have passed away.

Two years after I lost my mother, my brother died. I was married without either of them present. This would not be the end to my experience with loss. My husband and I had our fourth out of five children stillborn when I was just one day shy of 36 weeks along. My husband passed away a few years later after a short battle with stomach cancer, leaving me to raise our four children alone. Our oldest was 9 and the baby was just a year and a half. A year later my father's brother and best friend passed away and then just a few years later, my father joined them all in heaven. After my husband died, I was told I really should write. When people met me, they couldn't imagine my story went with my smile, my positive attitude. I was told that my ability to suffer loss and still live my life and truly be happy was an inspiration to many. So, in 2016, I started a blog. The response has been overwhelming. I have received many messages of people telling me that my stories give them hope of getting through their own tragedies. People started to thank me for writing and sharing my life. I decided to write about whatever it was I was thinking about or feeling, after all that's what real life is. I enjoy humor very much and laughter has always been a coping mechanism for my family. I like to give people hope, but also just to make them laugh sometimes. We all need a break from daily stress and sometimes all we can do is laugh. This book is a compilation of many of my blog entries from the past 5 years. They are presented in the order they were written. Some may make you laugh. Some may make you cry. Some may give you hope or inspire you. Some may just let you know you're not alone.

Anchored~

Bobby died on May 17th, 2015, after a 7-month battle with stomach cancer. We had been together for 15 years, married for nearly 11. We had been raising 4 beautiful, and still very young, children together. Previous to his passing, I had experienced losing loved ones too many times. I have learned too much at 40, lost too many people that I love. However, these lessons just keep making me stronger. I don't know why. I can only say God gave me a foundation in the way I was raised, amazing parents, to believe the good in the world and to be the good in the world. He also gave me a heart to never lose hope. It is my hope that I am passing that on to my own children.

Life is an ocean. We are the captain of our own ships, but we cannot control the weather. The storms will come and at times will be fierce, but they will also subside. We need to refuse to sink. We cannot drown in these waves. We need to ride them with everything we've got. We need to come out on top. One thing we can be guaranteed, is that the storms will also go away. We will be left in calm waters, sun shining, floating peacefully along. We need to remember that our boat can drop anchor, as can our lives. An anchor is a symbol of staying grounded, of not being pulled out to sea in these storms. We are our own anchor and hope is always an anchor for our soul!

My blog is titled, "Refuse to Sink" because I am an anchor for my family, keeping us grounded, but I also refuse to let our boat sink in the storms. I have been asked to write and publish for a while now. I think it is finally time. My experiences make me who I am, but we all have experiences, good and bad. I am not unique in that I have had to battle some pretty, shitty stuff.
We all do! No one person's problem is better or worse than another's. They are just different and not to be judged. It is what it is, but how will we sail our ship? How do we view the world? How do we get through these storms? If the way I live my life and my attitude and my smile after my own storms help even one person to have hope for their own future, then this book will

have served its purpose. I hope I will inspire my readers and, also make them laugh. Most of all, I hope that even if one of my blog entries makes you cry, it will also end leaving you with a smile on your face.

Greyson~

I felt Greyson kicking away in my tummy while I was eating my dish of mint chocolate chip ice cream. He was just as feisty as his 3 siblings had been in utero and it was great to watch his little feet and elbows (or whatever body part it was) pushing out in response to me poking him, like we all do. Like, "Hey, wake up Baby! But, remember to sleep in a little bit when I want to sleep!" And shortly after, I did go to sleep.

When I woke up the next morning at 6am, I knew I was in labor. I was just one day shy of 36 weeks, so I knew it wasn't that big of a deal. I had also planned on laboring at home for as long as possible, keeping in touch with my midwife, who agreed. Nothing abnormal was going on. I had done this already three times before. When 1pm hit, I was finally at the point when I knew I needed to get to the hospital, and we went. I was hooked up to the monitor and immediately was confused when they rolled in the ultrasound machine and the doctor came in to see why they couldn't find his heartbeat. My whole world changed in an instant when he told me we had lost him. No blood flow on the screen, no heartbeat, and no explanation. After never having drugs before, I begged them to knock me out and make sure I didn't feel a thing. It already wasn't fair, why should I also be in pain?

I still had to labor until 8pm when Greyson James Guay was stillborn, 4 lbs. 13 oz. I held him until my midwife gently let me know he would start to look different and I would want to remember him as he was when he was born and still looked alive.

That night was filled with such horrible heartbreak and anguish. It was also filled with angels. My nurses will forever have my gratitude and were put with me for a reason. They were amazing and gentle and kind. Having a friend in the same profession made me look back afterwards and realize how difficult their job must have been that night. I am sure they went into another room to cry and I know a few of them over the next 24 hours cried with me, as well. I tried to make sense of it all. I did every test I was supposed to, I exercised, I ate right, I didn't smoke or drink. Still, there was no reason, nothing to blame. Years before, I had lost my mom and my brother. Those experiences had made me angry with God and I lost a lot of faith. Over time, however, I saw God stand by me. I saw that even when my faith was gone, His love for me was not. He saw me through, using the people in my life as angels and guiding me to what I needed and where I needed to be. This time, loss was different because of the faith in me that had grown over time stronger than ever in my life. This time, I knew that God had somehow been working in good ways in my life and, that as heartbreaking as it was, God would get us through.

I had an amazing dream that night of my mom and my brother in heaven welcoming Greyson and holding him and thanking me for giving my mom her first grandchild she was able to hold and take care of for me since she had passed before the others had been born. I took comfort knowing it would be ok. Greyson was very appropriately buried with my mom and brother. But I know that was just his shell. He didn't need that body for his purpose. To all of you moms who have carried a stillborn, here is the most important thing I learned and I believe with all my heart and soul…. We were chosen. We were handpicked by God Himself. See, everyone needs to be born, even angels. We were blessed by God to carry an angel. (Or in some cases 2 or 3 angels!!) We were the lucky ones to feel an angel inside of us and to be able to give an angel such love, the love they would give back to this world 100 times more from the heavens! They were never meant to walk the earth, only to fly, and we were chosen to give them their wings. My children and I have an angel named Greyson and he is gorgeous, just like all your angels. I tell this to you because you need to know. You need to believe. You were not punished or jipped. You were chosen because of the love you have to give and the love you will always give, whether you choose to have more children or not. God will mend your heart. God will show you what you need when you need it. Meanwhile, hold your head high and talk to your angel all the time, knowing every day that you have been blessed.

Happy Birthday! ~

I never understood why some people complain about having birthdays and getting older. It especially bothers me when parents make comments about why their kids just keep growing up!

Birthdays in and of itself are the greatest gift we can receive! The chance to have lived another year, another day!! I love seeing my kids growing up and celebrating their birthdays!! They are here and alive and kicking!! In fact, I make a HUGE deal out of birthdays, celebrating for weeks that your very own New Year is here! This is a privilege denied to too many. I have seen many people lose their lives, and trust me, you want to get older, and hopefully, someday, be old!! You want to watch your kids hit milestones and become adults and be successful and, most importantly, healthy!!

This is the year where an entire group of some of my closest friends will all turn 40. I am honestly so excited to have made it this far and I pray for so many more birthdays. I have been blessed to have been married, have children, and have AMAZING friends. All of that happened, on top of an upbringing better than anyone could have ever asked for, with loving, giving parents that would do anything for me, my siblings, and all our friends. I have learned so much from my life, but mostly to be grateful and patient. There is always a silver lining and, whether we know it or not, it will come.

As I turn 40, I look at my blessings and my future with hope, love, and excitement for what it brings. I have plans!! Big plans!! And each year as I am granted yet another birthday and another chance to get even older, I will also be given more time for these accomplishments, goals, helping others, loving others, and, most importantly, and God willing, seeing my 4 amazing children get older and grow up too. So, Happy Birthday to all of us…grab your cane, hit your grandkids over the head with it, and be happy that your ship has yet to have sunk!!

Summah Time~

Today I was thinking about how much I LOVE summer. Yes, many of us do, but why? I have also met those winter lovers. I don't trust them. I mean, who really WANTS to be cold?!?!? I understand the lovers of fall. It's my second favorite season with its changing leaves, its crispness in the air, and its apple picking. I also can understand the spring lovers, even though the only reason I enjoy the rainy, nasty, still cold spring is because I know summer is coming.

Still, spring brings flowers and hope of those nice long, summer days. But then there it is, the love of summer and the big WHY? So, here's my take on it.

1. With the great weather and the longer days, we get outside more and we are more active. Vitamin D from the sun is important in so many ways. Being active is important for obvious reasons. It makes our bodies

feel good to move. Therefore, our minds feel good and we are happier!

2. Burgers, dogs, and the grill in general. Honestly, is there anything better than cooking on the grill? No mess in the kitchen and the food will almost always make everyone happy.

3. The smell of sunscreen. I could smell coconut ALL.DAY.LONG. Enough said.

4. We all look cooler in sunglasses.

5. The children can go outside and play. Even better, they can ride their bikes to their friends houses! For the first time all year, my house is quiet!

6. Gardens. Need I say more? As a homeschooler, it's the easiest lesson to teach because it teaches itself and it's fun. My kids don't have a clue that they have learned more science over the summer than they did during most of the year!! They also retain it and tell you all about it too!

7. Drinks. Fruity, girly, spritzy, pink drinks. Whip one of these out in the middle of January and you have

made EVERYBODY smile. Why? Because they are thinking of summer!

8. Music. There are so many great songs that all revolve around the summer and I want to listen to them and dance to them all winter to get me through.

9. The mentality. We go to bed late and don't care. Our kids stay up late and sleep late and we don't care. We eat ice cream every night and we don't care. We don't eat dinner until 7 or 8 because we were on the beach all day and we still don't care!

10. Here is my very favorite thing about the summer: I don't know what day it is almost ever and I DON'T CARE! Isn't it the best when you actually forget what day it is? Or when you only know the day because you have special plans that day?

Maybe it's just me, but although I try to embrace each day all year, I find the summertime makes it even more fun. If you love summer as much as I do, then let's try to hold onto it for as long as we can. Everyone is invited for margaritas at my house in January!! Let's grill up some burgers, crank the heat up to 80, lather the fake tanner, put on our sundresses, play a little Fresh Prince's 'Summertime', and maybe even forget the day of the week.

Thank you~

I wake up each day and put one foot in front of the other. I hope for the best and try not to think of what could go wrong. Some days it's easy. Some days, not so much.

But, know what makes it easier? People.

My kids and I are very blessed that we get help from friends and family whenever they can. That help is so important. When a friend comes and watches my kids so I can escape, it's appreciated. When my dad came and watched them so I was able to grocery shop alone, I was grateful. When someone offers to help me clean, I'm floored. When someone comes over in the middle of the night for me to take one kid to the hospital when she needs to go, instead of all four, that's so, so amazing. When a friend's husband and son carry 15-20 bags of pellets in from my shed in the winter so I don't have to do it again, well, yay!! When someone drops off dinner…I LOVE YOU.

But seriously, NONE of those reasons is the one single thing that keeps my head up and pushes me to keep doing what I'm doing, even when I'm so tired and so very weary.

I don't know why, but people keep telling me that I'm an inspiration to them. They tell me seeing my strength is the thing that keeps THEM going. I used to think they were just being nice and blowing smoke up my ass actually. But lately, I wonder, "What if they are being honest? What if watching me do what I need to do and push through and smile as much as humanly possible and keep my faith in God…. what if me living my life one foot in front of the other really is inspiring another person not to give up?!?!? Well, then I certainly can't stop!! In fact, I need to be even better every.single.day. so, they never give in or give up. Now, obviously, I'm human. We all are and we all have "those days". On "those days" we must reach even deeper to find that thing inside of us, that one small thing that may really, truly be inspiring another individual to keep going. When someone tells me I'm an inspiration or that I'm strong, I must do better. They are inspiring me to make sure I never let them down. They don't realize how much they are picking me up. Some days I just can't seem to find that pick me up. Then, suddenly, there they are. There is my fan club who don't even know they are my fan club! Thank you to my friends and to strangers, thank you. You certainly do make me feel like a rock star.

Warriors~

I do a lot of reflecting when it comes to most situations and this weekend was no different. In fact, the company made it impossible to not stop, look around, and take it all in. Most people that know me, know that my oldest daughter has an autoimmune disease and her body attacks everything, including her own blood cells. This has made her transfusion dependent since 2012. We are treated by an amazing staff at Hasbro Children's Hospital's Tomorrow Fund Clinic for Hematology and Oncology in Providence. We are there once a week. We have also met many other families there at clinic. These people have become another family to us. The children play together there in the waiting/play room. They do arts and crafts, play games, and keep each other distracted as much as possible from why they are there in the first place. The parents become close very quickly as well. We know each other's stories all too well since we are all living a very similar one. We share a common bond. We worry about our children in a way that others don't understand. Our expenses and time are taken up in a way others are not, but we don't care as long it helps our kids. We know medical terminology that we wish we didn't. We can talk with doctors like it's nobody's business. We aren't out to impress anyone; we just know too much. We listen to our children tell us it's not fair that they feel crappy or that they have to miss out on something that their friends or siblings get to do because they are in a hospital for a day, a week, a month.

There are many activities that the clinic sponsors or gets us information about that are outside of the clinic. They do an amazing job of giving these kids and their families fun times. This past weekend, however, a bunch of clinic mommas decided to do a beach day and cookout at my house together. I am blessed to live in a beautiful area across the street from an amazing beach. So, Sunday, we got seven mom's and 20 children together, 7 of them having already kicked their diseases ass or in the middle of kicking it.

Seven Little Amazing Warriors. Seven Strong Warrior Mommas. Thirteen Wonderful Sweet Siblings. Instead of being attached to IV poles, they were attached to boogie boards. Instead of filtered hospital air, they were breathing in the smell of salt and sunscreen. Running down the hallways was replaced with running in the sand. There were smiles and laughter and there was loud, real loud. These kids know how to live it up better than any other kids I know and watching them do it was not taken lightly by any of us. We moms watched with gratitude that this day, this memory was happening. We all know how quickly life can change. We stare a little longer, smile a little differently, hug a little harder. We love these kids, not only our own, but each of these children. We pray for them all. We do what we can to help each other. We get it. Without saying a word, we all get it. We will always have a bond. We all, without a doubt, would go back to the blissful ignorance we once knew before our kid's diagnoses, but we also know that we are in the presence of greatness. We have each other. We love each other. We are the strongest group of mommas in the world. We know how blessed we are to have had this weekend. We know how blessed we are to have each other. And we know how blessed we are to have our children. Our warriors will continue to be amazing. Fight on little warriors. Mommas got your back.

Widow Dating~

My husband passed away May 17, 2015. Before that, he fought cancer for 7 months. It was a long, ugly battle filled with more dark times, yelling, anger, depression and sadness than I could have ever imagined. But it was also filled with apologies, time to discuss difficult topics nobody wants to think about, saying things that needed to be said, and love.

Every situation and every marriage are different. People are different. I always look at the glass as full, not half-full, but totally filled with love and joy and God's blessings everyday. Bobby's glass was unfortunately always empty and that made fighting cancer hard, so very hard. It also made for a difficult marriage. I fell in love with my husband and never lost that love, no matter what we went through. I prayed for him and for us and our children and I always had hope that we could all be happy together, that the depression and anger would go away.

Then, he was diagnosed with stage 4 gastric cancer. We went through all of the suggested chemo, diet, etc. We had wonderful friends and family who couldn't have been more supportive.
We did everything right, but God's plan is always bigger than our own. Bobby was a good man.

There is no doubt about that. He helped people whenever he could, he worked hard, he loved his kids and me to the moon and back. He was hilarious and outgoing. Some of the good friends I have now were his friends first and I am blessed that he had a personality that attracted good people. We had some great times together and I am blessed to have friends and family that will talk about those good times and keep all the good memories alive for our children. It's impossible to go back and change the past, but he did make the future easier for me in a few ways. He tied up loose ends and had the courage to talk about what I was facing as a single mom of 4. We talked about finances, house issues, the children, and me dating again. I couldn't even imagine another man in my life and didn't want to talk about it. He apologized for so many things and told me to promise him that I would find someone to sweep me off my feet and make me happy. I told him to just shut up! At the time, I didn't want to think about it. I also have always had great faith in God and know He will take care of me.

When the smoke cleared, I did decide to start being good to myself and get out and meet new people. I just wanted to have fun and not think too hard about what would come of it. And that's what I did. I focused on enjoying the life I have been given to the fullest.

When you lose your spouse, your head spins and it doesn't stop for quite some time. Even after years, there are still duties of running a household that I need to get under control, but I know I am getting closer every day. I get rather impatient, but need to remind myself that with 4 children and being a single mom, shit will just take time to get done!

I know there are other young widows out there that struggle with the same issues in dating. Here is what I've come up with. While I take time for myself and spend time with friends and family who care about me and make me laugh, I also get a big kick out of dating. I enjoy meeting new people and being social. And almost everyone in my life is supportive.

I think we should all do what is right for each of us. I don't believe there is a magic time for when dating is or isn't ok again. It depends on you and what will make YOU happy. I think so many widows feel guilty when they date again, but here is why I don't think we should.

I lost my mom almost 17 years ago. Since then, I have found 3 women I can go to on a regular basis for advice or help or just to be there as company. They are all older, near my mom's age, and they are all very motherly to me. This does not mean that any of them have replaced my mom or become my mom. I will only ever have 1 mom, but these women have filled a void in my life that nobody should have to go without. They love me and help me and I love them for who they are to me. I am grateful for their presence and what they have brought to my life, both for me and for my children. Similarly, when my brother passed away 15 years ago, many of his friends stepped in to fill the 'big brother' void. They are still part of my life and in a big way. My brothers' friends became my friends. They still look out for me, check on me, and are here to protect me as well, like a big brother should. I don't know what I would do without these men in my life. None of them will ever replace my brother, but they are also filling a void for me. They have taken over a job and stepped up to love me like a sister. Again, I am nothing but grateful for their love and support (even if they still tease me like I'm 10!).

Finding a partner in life is no different, in my opinion. There will never be another Bobby. And, to all widows, your partner will never be replaced. Like my mom and my brother, they are people we will always miss. But, it's ok for us to have someone in our lives that provides what we had. In fact, it's more than ok! We need and deserve to find that love again! It's more than ok for us to enjoy fun, companionship, support, and adventures again with someone. Life is not meant to be lived alone. Do what you need to do in your own time. Listen to your own heart, not others judgements. And never feel guilty for getting back out into the world and enjoying some fun!! Dress up, make yourself smell nice, and hire a babysitter. You will be surprised what a few hours out will do, especially for a single parent!!

Things I Want My Kids to Know~

1. EVERYBODY HAS THEIR SHIT.

As you go through life, there will be ups and downs. You are not the only one who will experience the downs. Other people may have different battles to fight than you, but everybody has them. You do not deserve anyone's pity, nor should you want it. Pity gets you nowhere fast. Cry about it. Feel bad for a bit. Then, pick yourself up. Or, better yet, do what I do and surround yourself with amazing friends who will help you pick yourself up and see the good all around you.

2. ENJOY THE UPS.

Yes, there will be downs, but there will also be ups. Cherish them!! When you hear the saying,

"Life is like a roller coaster," it is not a joke!! The good times and bad times will always come and go. Don't be a pessimist and wait for the next bad time. Assume instead that it will be ages away and enjoy the good to the very fullest extent. Revel in it!

3. SEEK MORE GOOD.

Even when times are tough, think of as many good things in your life as you can. I promise you, it will not only change your mood, but it will make you see more good than you realized. When you seek the good, it grows more good in your life. Try it!! You have nothing to lose!!

4. YOU WILL NOT WIN EVERYTHING.

A trophy for every kid. Ugh. This one gets me every time. We all have different talents. We are all unique. Find what you love to do and do your best. I love to run. It makes me feel good. I have never won first place in a race. That's ok. If you really like the thing you want to win in, and you really want to win, then try harder and practice more. If you keep at it, you will reach your goal. Just know that you are good enough in life, even if you come in last in the mile.

5. STAY TRUE TO YOURSELF

Decide who you are and what you enjoy and want out of life. Then build from that. Don't let what others have or like influence you because in the end you won't be living your own life and you won't be happy. Don't set out to hurt people and know there are times you need to compromise with others, especially in relationships, but never compromise what means the most to you in life and NEVER compromise your morals.

6. LAUGH!!!!!

If you can't laugh at yourself, I promise you I always will! Learn to crack a joke, whenever it could ease the tension (which is almost always!). I cannot tell you the number of times I have laughed through tears. It doesn't make the situation go away, but it relieves a little stress and many times helps you to refocus on the good. I have been blessed to surround myself with people that know it's ok to make me laugh and crack jokes as well, no matter how shitty it's going. Those people are your tribe!!

7. TAKE CARE OF YOUR TRIBE!!

Speaking of your tribe, love them! Your tribe consists of the people you surround yourself with and call your friends. They can be family too, of course. They support you and know you inside and out. They say the right thing at the right time and when they don't, you know them so well that it doesn't matter. Take care of these relationships. Life is hard. You might not always be in a position to do something big for someone else, but remember that a text or phone call just checking in means a lot too. Good friends know you don't need to talk everyday to support one another. You can count on good friends, but also make sure that they know they can count on you too! There have been times in my own life that I have had so much to handle, that I wished more than anything I could just stop and go to a friend and help them. I could at least call and check in and be a shoulder if they needed it. And then, there will be times when you can be there 100% for someone else- DO IT!! Don't ever take your tribe for granted.

8. STAY ACTIVE

You will always feel better about yourself (no matter how much you weigh) and your current situation, if you stay active and exercise. Take care of your body. It's the only one you have.
God gave it to you, and you are amazing!!

9. ALWAYS BE NICE

There is never a reason to be nasty, even when you really want to be. Let others act how they choose. This is not being fake. I'm not saying invite your enemies over for a tea party. I'm saying that if you must spend time or have a conversation with someone you don't really like, just literally grin and bear it. If someone insults you or hurts your feelings, you have every right to tell them. However, do not attack them back. It does no good to you or to them. Be the bigger person.

10. GO FOR IT

Never tried snowboarding before? Throw on a helmet and give it a whirl! Afraid to go on that date in case it just doesn't work out? Dress yourself up, have a blast, and think positive! Nervous to start a new career or endeavor. Put one foot in front of the other and take it from there! Whatever opportunities you have, take them! Whatever you want out of life, go get it! A few people laugh at me when I throw out the term YOLO. For those of you that don't know, it means, "You Only Live Once". Yes!! This is it, no dress rehearsal, no second chance! There will be critics, but who cares? You are meant to LIVE and to DO in your life. (Obviously there are exceptions like dangerous, stupid stuff, but I'm assuming here that common sense is involved in decision making.) So, wear what you want, have your own opinions, speak up, but be nice, and take those chances that come your way!

Moms I Don't Get~

So, after a day like today, where I can't do anything right for my kids and we are late everywhere (as usual) and I didn't accomplish even a small portion of what was on my 'to do' list (again, as usual), I thought about this Mommin' job and what makes it work. So, here is a list of moms I would NOT relate to at all….

1. Mom's who don't drink. How? Don't your children drive you crazy? I mean, obviously drinking everyday is out of the question and overdoing it is out of the question, but once in a while it just.makes.sense.

2. Mom's who don't yell. Again, how? The most common scenario in my house is that I ask nicely about 125 times. Nobody listens. I then scream... Everybody looks horrified and sometimes cry. Then they ask me why I had to yell…. REALLY?!?

3.   Mom's who don't swear….Because guess what? When the baby craps his pants just as we are leaving the house, it's not just literally a shitshow, it's a f**king shitshow.

4.   Moms with clean houses. Do you live there. Where is all your stuff? You make me feel messy and we can't be friends…unless you'd like to clean my house. Then we can be best friends.

5.   Mom's who look put together. Don't you own yoga pants? Don't you know how comfy they are? How did you have a chance to blow dry your hair today AND put on makeup? How have your tween girls not taken and destroyed all of your makeup anyways?!?

6.   Moms with clean cars. You MUST have other moms pick up your children and bring them places for you. Children are gross little people that leave wrappers and lollipops where ever they go…. Do you seriously

have time more than once or twice a year to see what's under those car seats??

7.   Mom's who are organized. This is a pipe dream people. I suppose there was a time I was organized when I had one baby... bahahaha!! How do you keep track of what every kid needs for school and activities? Isn't it enough that I feed them?!?

8.   Mom's who cook every.single.night. Don't get me wrong, I love to cook and bake. I would do much more of it if I could. How do you manage to make dinner every night with kid's activities and just being stinkin' exhausted? And when you do make dinner, how do you cover ALL the food groups? Can we consider a muffin for lunch healthy? I mean, it's not a cupcake... even if it is a chocolate muffin....

9.   Mom's who don't laugh. These little shits drive me nuts all day long, but they do some seriously messed up stuff. If I didn't make light of it, I would just bang my head against the wall. They are like little shitty

comedians. Really, they should have their own show…and make mama some money while they're at it!

10. Mom's who don't hug and cuddle. At the end of the day, when these guys have me losing my voice, replacing every word in my vocabulary with an f bomb, and finishing another bottle of wine, I still know they are the most awesome little brats on the face of the earth. The greatest feeling in the world that melts all that other crap away are those hugs!!

Let it Go~

The term "let it go" might be a little different from person to person, but the concept is the same. When some people let things go, they just remind themselves that it's life and they need to roll with the punches. Some people do some partying and try to forget about what they can't change.

Then others, like myself, let it go by giving the 'it' to God. I take a deep breath, let it out and try to imagine God removing the stress and weight from my shoulders and, literally, taking it away. In any account, in order to let go of something, we need to believe that we are not in control of all things, whether you believe in God or the universe or karma or whatever. Focusing only on changing what we can control and working on controlling our reaction over situations we can't is key to letting things go.

I really think letting things go has got to be the hardest, yet most rewarding thing we can do next to becoming a parent. When you become a parent, you understand that it really is the toughest job you'll ever love. As we go through life, I'm certain the same can be said for just letting go.

This is also one of those things that is most definitely easier said than done! I don't believe anyone could ever do it 100% of the time and in every situation. I am getting better at it as life goes on, but sometimes it is much harder to do than other times! Let's take, for example, this week. It has been no less than challenging and my patience for a challenge has worn thin. Oh, and it's only Wednesday!

So, here's what I do (after I whine to my best friends, visit pity party land, then return to what I still know is my blessed life). I take each situation separately because all the shit little things that seem to happen all at once are overwhelming, but easier to reason one by one. Then I do just that…I reason with myself.

The power went out and when it came back on my computer and four of my lights wouldn't work. One of the lights was in the kitchen so my children had to make school lunches by my phone light. The next day they all started working again 15 minutes before the electrician showed up! So...did I do anything to cause this situation? Nope. Did we check all of the fuses? Yup. Could I control this? Nope. Now, let's look at the good. Did you see how I said, "MY CHILDREN had to make school lunches by my phone light"? Yes! That's right! I did NOT need to make their lunches because my girls, grades 4 and 6 are perfectly capable of making their own and they do! I know for a fact some of my friends would pay good money not to make lunches every.single.night. And the electrician didn't charge for coming out because he just had to tighten a few wires!

Same night...Hanna says, "What are those little black things jumping on Cocoa's legs?" The dog has fleas. Awesome. My fault? Again, nope. Can I fix this at 9pm? Negative. The next day I call the groomer who

takes her for a flea bath. Meanwhile, I start cleaning my house at
7am. Stripping things, scrubbing things, vacuuming things. Between picking kids up and dinner

I finish cleaning duties at 8pm. I'm exhausted and want to roll up in a ball and cry. But…. I was able to clean out the playroom and get rid of a huge bin and trash bag worth of crap my kids don't play with anymore while the 4th grader is at school and can't protest. My living room is spotless, cleaner than its been in months! Oh, and it wouldn't have been possible without the help of my amazing 6-year-old. Yes, be jealous again…I have a 6-year-old boy who cleans and helps his mama! Talk about being blessed! I had been wanting to get to that for a while, so, at the end of the day the dog and the house are clean! (The children…not so much, but baths can wait until morning!)

So, here's the toughest one to turn around, but if anyone can do it, I can. This morning I get a phone call from school that my daughter who is transfusion dependent on platelets has a nosebleed. Ugh. I had just stepped out of the shower, 2-year-old not dressed and hungry, and my head spinning. I make it out of the house in 17 minutes (which, if you know me, is amazing). I get to the school and I know she is shaken, but my amazing kid is only showing her brave face. I can see the look in her eyes though. I'm her mom. I know her. I smile and rub her back and she tells me she has a blood clot stuck in her throat. We get the bucket and call the hospital to let them know we will be there in 45 minutes for platelets because chances are it won't stop bleeding until she gets them. She starts throwing up blood clots on the way to Providence and crying about how much her tummy hurts. We get about 25 minutes away and we see the bumper-to-bumper traffic not.moving.at.all. I pop the address into the GPS to see what's going on. A rollover and 25-minute delay. Ugh again. The GPS tells me to exit and the map shows me going through a city to get back on the highway at an exit right after the accident. I take the back roads and get to the on ramp for the highway to see it is closed due to the rollover happening where the ramp meets the highway! So, I need to drive back around the other way to get back on the highway and then I drive like a complete ass in the breakdown lane and cut people off knowing they'd understand and do it too if it were their own kid. We get through it and finally to the clinic. Platelets are ready. My poor girl has a yucky tummy and her nose is still bleeding. In total it bleeds for 3 1/2 hours. She is scared to even check the tissue to see if it stopped, but finally does and we are able to head home after a 7-hour total trip. On the way home, 6-year-old Brody says, "Mom, don't you wish we never had to go to Hasbro?" Well, that made me think!

This was my answer. I am eternally grateful that science has come so far as to be able to give

Joni red blood cells and platelets when she needs them. Without them, she wouldn't be here. But she is. And she is thriving. She competes in gymnastics and practices 9 hours a week. She loves gym and is an excellent student. She loves her family and her friends. She has fun and we are so blessed to be able to be a part of it all. Without the staff at the hospital that does everything and anything we need and goes above and beyond for us; we would be in a much worse situation as well. By going there, we have become friends with some of the most wonderful, caring women and men on earth. If we hadn't gone today, we also wouldn't have run into some of our best friends. We got to have an impromptu visit with friends we don't get to see too often. What a surprise blessing!

Ok, so there it is. I reasoned. Now I can let it go. Like I said, it's not always easy, but totally worth it. I couldn't control any of these situations, but it is now in the past and done. It is what it is and tomorrow is another day. Think about what's weighing you down. Can you control it?
Can you change it? If the answer is NO, then just LET IT GO! If I can do this, so can you!

Mike~

This post is written from excerpts of an essay I wrote about my brother back when I was in college. He passed away on October 10, 2003 and it still takes my breath away to think of how much I miss him.

I was not an easy child. Detachment was always a problem. Looking back, I am surprised that I never drove my mother to drink. I do not remember a specific first day of school. What I do remember are two years of violent temper tantrums. When I was a first grader at Elizabeth Pole Elementary School, my brother, Mike, was in 5th grade. The teachers would pull him out of his classroom to come calm me down when I had one of my fits. It was reassuring to me to have him there.

My teacher was about nine feet tall. She believed in toughening children up right from the start. We were afraid of her ruler and her threat to "shake us up" if we behaved badly. One would think that this fear would subside upon beginning second grade in Ms. O'Brien's room. After all, she was only 4 feet tall! However, second grade was worse than I could have imagined. My brother was now at a new school. I was on my own! I may have been scared as a child, but I still had guts for a seven-year-old. We used to walk to school. It didn't take me long to realize that I could just walk back home before I reached the school's front door. I would watch my friends go into the building. Then, I would turn around and be gone. Oh, to see my mother's face when I walked back into the door just a few minutes after I had left!

Looking back, the most frightening thing about second grade was being without my brother. By having my brother close by, I was calmed. I didn't really overcome my detachment issues as I aged. When it was time to go away to college, I was excited and a little nervous, as any eighteen-year-old would be. I chose to go away to the University of Connecticut. It took me about a month to realize that this being away from home thing was not all it was cracked up to be. Now, twelve years later, I would rely on the comfort of my brother again. Of course, the phone bill was tremendous, as cell phone service was quite different in 1994 as it is now, and he was going to college in Virginia at the time. As in first grade, I called on him to make my experience easier. I trusted my big brother's advice. I called him when I wanted to know what mixed best with vodka. Then, I called him when I wanted to know what to do about my hangover. I also called him when I was homesick and crying and I did not want to worry my mom and dad.

When we are upset, overwhelmed, scared, sad, etc., we call on those we trust and love to help us through. Mike and I fought a lot as kids, but we also loved each other very much and when push came to shove, I knew he would always help out his little sister. Losing him was so difficult in many ways, but I definitely miss what we didn't get to have together the most. I didn't get to see him at my wedding. I didn't get to see him hold my babies. I know he would have been the coolest uncle ever and it really sucks that my kids don't have him in their lives. Most of all, I miss that positive support I know he would have given me through the tough times. We talk about him all the time, especially the funny stories because there are so many! I also see him reflected in a lot of ways in my kids. His quirky personality traits come through here and there and I know he is getting a good laugh over it. I may not have him physically by my side, but I know he is always with my kids, and me. And, the odds are, he's probably farting.

Love you Michael David Fernandes, February 5, 1972- October 10, 2003

Yuletide Cheer~

I live in New England. We are used to changing seasons and I do think they are all beautiful in their own way, but I am really a summer girl. I love the sun and the warmth. So, when daylight savings kicks in that first week of November, I need to make some adjustments.

It's dark out. It's not even 5 effing o'clock and it's dark out. Oh, it's also 42 degrees out and dark. Did I mention it's already DARK?? I've already eaten dinner for Pete's sake and not even to get an early bird special!! It just felt like I should eat because it was getting DARK. Ugh. (This must be why we all get fat in the winter.) So, not sure you remember, but about 8 weeks ago we were still going to the beach. It was sunny there. Actually, it was still sunny there
MUCH later than 5 effing o'clock! As the fall has hit and now the colder weather, anyone like me is screwed. I hate winter. I hate being cold. I really, really miss the hot, sweaty sun. My body and brain most definitely miss

the vitamin D. By now, whatever amount my body stored is gone. The wonderful vitamin D from the wonderful sun that I spend so much time outside enjoying is now gone. The seasonal depression could set in like it does for so many. Except, it won't. It's not my wonderful, glass full attitude that will ward it off. Its not the counting down until summer returns either. It's my focus.

Halloween is over. Its November. I don't care what anyone else decides. For me and my family, the magical, blessed holiday season has begun!! We all need to stop that depression from coming, but how? By celebrating!! I try to forget that it's cold and dark and I'm eating too much chocolate. Instead, there's a new focus.... CHRISTMAS!! Or honestly whatever holiday you celebrate!! It's just a great time to reflect on the many benefits of this season of GIVING!!

Now I hear all of you grinches out there and I know some of you are my very best friends even!!

But stop being grinches!! There's plenty of times in life you can concentrate on the negative in a situation, but that has never gotten us anywhere, has it? No! There is nothing wrong with getting really excited about a time of year you love and sharing that excitement with people you love!

So, here are my top 10 favorite things about the holiday season:

1. Presence. No, not presents, presence. There are parties. Lots of parties. Which means people, people we probably haven't seen since last year. Now I understand we all know people we aren't psyched to see and have to anyways, but there are so many people in my own life that I just don't see enough! I love my family and friends. I think about them more often than they know. Life is so busy, but at the holidays we make time to see each other and I love it!!

2. Elf (and all other Christmas movies!). It doesn't matter what religion you are…how can you not love

Will Farrell and his performance in the movie Elf? I could watch this anytime, even July. It will never get old!

3. Good deeds. We should do good deeds all year long, obviously. I do what I can when I can regardless of the season. But whether it be the media attention or just a feeling in the air, we see more good deeds done during the holiday season than any other time of year. This makes me feel great! I love to see people smiling and the unexpected, wonderful things we can do for one another makes people happy.

4. Gag gifts. Laughing is my favorite. What better way to laugh than to give a loved one a fart in a bag or anal beads in their stocking? Come on, you know it's funny!

5. "Santa! I know him!" So, I really do…I believe in Santa. I don't care if you think I'm crazy. Most of my friends figured that out years ago. St. Nicholas was a real person a very long time ago. Yes, he has since

passed away, but he left a legacy! He left giving to loved ones, strangers, those in need, etc. as a legacy. He left a magic in the air that if you just close your eyes and allow yourself, you'll feel it too!

6. Christmas lights. Picture Clark's house in National Lampoons Christmas Vacation when the lights finally work! Yes! I'm with him! You can't have too many lights! It's dark and cold out as you pull into your neighborhood, but your house looks so inviting and fun and cozy because it's all lit up like the 4th of July! Just. Awesome.

7. Food! Omg...we can't possibly forget the FOOD! I love to cook and bake and entertain! It has always amazed me that a smell or a taste can take you back to a memory. Just close your eyes. My mom handed me down so many wonderful recipes and traditions that I get to share now with my own children and our friends and family. I love when I make something she always made and old friends and family members tell me it's just like they remember it and it

brings them back to our old Christmas parties that my mom used to host. She isn't here anymore physically, but it's the best way I know to keep her always in the heart of every Christmas for all of us!

8. Children. If you ever doubt the magic of the holiday season or you need to get a wake up call on its wonder and blessings, just look at a child! Watch them as it gets closer. Yes, they can get off the wall when they get over-stimulated, but they are so stinkin' excited! Spend a little time looking at it all through their eyes. It's contagious!

9. Mail! Who doesn't love good, old-fashioned snail mail? Seriously, admit it! You run to the mailbox like a kid everyday and can't wait to see something that's not a bill! It's a card that's telling you to have a great holiday and a wonderful new year! Isn't that thoughtful? Yes! And the pictures! I love the pictures! I love seeing everyone getting so big and I love seeing the families and the single people with their dogs even! It's all good! You are on many people's card sending

lists…now send them yourself! Don't act like it's a pain, just do it and make other people smile because you gave them fun mail!

10. Christmas Music! There are very few genres of music that can be sung by several generations and everyone knows the words! Unless you're singing twisted carols, they are appropriate and clean and send fun, playful, and sweet messages. If you are listening to the twisted carols, well sometimes that's even better! Who doesn't enjoy a good parody? Some years, my children and I have gone caroling in our neighborhood with our friends. It is so much fun! I highly recommend everyone at some point in time get over yourself and just go outside and sing! Who cares what you sound like? Carols are for everyone!

So, there you go! These are great reasons to embrace the holiday season! Of course, you don't have to get into it yet if you don't want to, but then you can't escape my holiday spirit anytime you see me! Plus, I know you really love me no matter how crazy you think I am.

Mahalo~

Well, I suppose when you write a blog, you need to join the masses and put your "Grateful for..." list out there to the world. I'm pretty much the most grateful person I know. I definitely have tons of reasons to say, "Thank you!". So here are just a few... *My kids. They are awesome little shits!

My tween 11-year-old drives me crazy in so many ways and I don't put up with much of her attitude. However, she also spends some time every week at the hospital getting poked and prodded and has been nothing less than a champion in my eyes. Tween/teen years are hard for everyone, but under that sass I have one cool young lady.

I have a quirky 9-year-old that won't put up with anyone's bullshit. She's got looks to kill, which I secretly love if she doesn't use them on me. She always sees the bright side at the end of her tantrums.

I have a 6-year-old son that cooks and cleans. He makes his own eggs, his among other specialties. This week while I was running on our treadmill, he made chicken soup from scratch all by himself and did one heck of a job. He said he thought it would make a good lunch!

I have a sweet, stubborn, independent 3-year-old that climbs in my lap and smiles and makes me forget that he just spilled a gallon of apple juice on the couch.

Pubby. That's what my kids call my dad. If he didn't help drive my kids around, I don't know what I would do. We would never have a home cooked meal since they have something nearly every night. And they would never have a normal bedtime. Siblings would be dragged everywhere and I know they are starting to hate that too. He does so much more for me and my kids, but driving just pops into my head because I just can't be in two spots at once!

Friends. Shit, I'm spoiled. I know it. I am so grateful. I know they don't want anything in return, but when I win the lottery, I am sharing!!

My Jeep. Sure, it sounds materialistic, but it's more of a symbol for me of just so many things. My friends know. I know they get it. It's me. It's a part of who I am and always will be and it represents a link to the past and who I'm becoming as I'm still learning on this crazy ride called
life.

Last, but definitely not least, I am ever so grateful that Thanksgiving is done and I will have less friends that complain when I'm all about spreading my Christmas cheer!! So, no more Bah Humbug…let the Holiday season begin!!

A Mom's Twelve Days of Christmas~ You know the tune….

On the first day of Christmas, my children gave to me:

A hunk of poop under the Christmas tree!

On the second day of Christmas, my children gave to me:

2 pairs of underwear on the couch and a hunk of poop under the Christmas tree!

On the third day of Christmas, my children gave to me:

3 cases of strep throat, 2 pairs of underwear on the couch, and a hunk of poop under the Christmas tree!

On the fourth day of Christmas, my children gave to me:

4 children fighting, 3 cases of strep throat, 2 pairs of underwear on the couch, and a hunk of poop under the Christmas tree!

On the fifth day of Christmas, my children gave to me:

5 hours of sleep!

4 children fighting, 3 cases of strep throat, 2 pairs of underwear on the couch, and a hunk of poop under the Christmas tree!

On the sixth day of Christmas, my children gave to me:

6 empty Capri Sun wrappers on the floor

5 hours of sleep!

4 children fighting, 3 cases of strep throat, 2 pairs of underwear on the couch, and a hunk of poop under the Christmas tree!

On the seventh day of Christmas, my children gave to me:

7 days a week of activities
6 empty Capri Sun wrappers on the floor
5 hours of sleep!

4 children fighting, 3 cases of strep throat, 2 pairs of underwear on the couch, and a hunk of poop under the Christmas tree!

On the eighth day of Christmas, my children gave to me:

8 rolling eyes

7 days a week of activities, 6 empty Capri Sun wrappers on the floor,

5 hours of sleep!

4 children fighting, 3 cases of strep throat, 2 pairs of underwear on the couch, and a hunk of poop under the Christmas tree!

On the ninth day of Christmas, my children gave to me:

9 socks without a match

8 rolling eyes, 7 days a week of activities, 6 empty Capri Sun wrappers on the floor,

5 hours of sleep!

4 children fighting, 3 cases of strep throat, 2 pairs of underwear on the couch, and a hunk of poop under the Christmas tree!

On the tenth day of Christmas, my children gave to me:

10 loads of laundry each week

9 socks without a match, 8 rolling eyes, 7 days a week of activities, 6 empty Capri Sun wrappers on the floor

5 hours of sleep!

4 children fighting, 3 cases of strep throat, 2 pairs of underwear on the couch, and a hunk of poop under the Christmas tree!

On the eleventh day of Christmas, my children gave to me:

11 episodes of Paw Patrol

10 loads of laundry each week, 9 socks without a match, 8 rolling eyes, 7 days a week of activities, 6 empty Capri Sun wrappers on the floor

5 hours of sleep!

4 children fighting, 3 cases of strep throat, 2 pairs of underwear on the couch, and a hunk of poop under the Christmas tree!

On the twelfth day of Christmas, my children gave to me:

12 Months a year of LOVE! (Even though they can be little assholes)

11 episodes of Paw Patrol, 10 loads of laundry each week, 9 socks without a match, 8 rolling eyes, 7 days a week of activities, 6 empty Capri Sun wrappers on the floor

5 hours of sleep!

4 children fighting, 3 cases of strep throat, 2 pairs of underwear on the couch….AND A HUNK

OF POOP UNDER THE CHRISTMAS TREE!!

Mom~

My mother passed away December 23, 2001. I remember every detail of that day and the next. I remember being with her right as she passed. I remember the visitors, my friends not saying a word because there was nothing to say. They just brought me mint chocolate chip ice cream and jimmies like any best friends would have done. I remember needing to have a Christmas tree up and decorated, for her. I remember my brother and I and two of our friends going to pick one out. It was more important to me than anyone could understand. I don't think I even truly understood why it was so important to me, but now, 15 years later, I do.

My mother loved Christmas. She gave me a love for the holiday that I will always cherish and hand down to my own children. She shopped early, we listened to Christmas music together in the car by the end of September, and she always had her wonderful Christmas party.

Thanksgiving night was more special to me than the entire day because that's the night we would put out the nativity- our first Christmas decoration up every year.

Christmas eve at church was always my mom and I, usually with my aunt and my cousin. The men all worked together and had their annual holiday party at the furniture store. I remember her singing "Oh Come All Ye Faithful" just a bit off key. I loved that song and still do. Christmas eve mass was always something special and I have yet to sit through an entire one since the year she died without crying like a baby at some point.

Christmas morning, I woke up before my siblings every year. My brother was always the last one up, especially when he was in high school and college. My mom had a rule that we couldn't wake him up until 9 to open presents! We all had to wait to go into the living room until all three of us were up and ready and my dad had this video camera rolling. Once everyone was up, we opened our stockings and then went to work on the gifts under the tree. I don't really remember the stuff, but I do remember the magic that went along with it all. I can even still see the excitement on my parents faces, awaiting our own expressions.

The memories my mother gave me will always be important, but they are especially precious to me at Christmas time. I know everything happens for a reason. I don't know why she had to be taken from us so soon, but I do know her passing two days before Christmas was her way of making sure I always keep her memory alive at her favorite time of year. I love every second of this season, celebrating, not just Christmas, but honoring my mom. The smells of her recipes, the stories that I tell my children, and the special homemade decorations that she made are all ways to have her extra close to me at a time when I miss her the most.

I believe that when you all of a sudden have something you want to tell someone who is in heaven and you actually have a moment where you want to call them, that it just means they are so close you really could talk to them. It means they are there with you. Two nights ago, Hanna, my 9-year-old, asked to help me make my mother's special Christmas bread. I showed her how to knead it and braid it. I walked away and she did one all by herself and it looked amazing.

When I told her so, she replied, "Grandma Joan must have been working through my hands and helping me to make it perfect!" I immediately wanted to call her because I knew she would be so proud of the job Hanna did on her first try. Hanna and I both decided that my mom must have been right there beside us, watching, helping, and most definitely proud.

I am so proud of the people that my children are becoming. I get complimented on them often. I know that it would be impossible for me to raise great kids if I wasn't raised by such great parents. I am so grateful for all they did for me, but I am most grateful for the memories that I will always share. Fifteen years later and it still takes my breath away. Life isn't always fair, but we need to accept the ways we are blessed and hold those memories and stories close. Thank you, Mom, for helping to make me who I am and, most definitely for giving me my love of Christmas!

Please don't feel bad for me~

Tonight, my daughter and I got our "15 minutes of fame". She has an autoimmune disorder and her body attacks itself. This means her body creates antibodies against her own blood cells, killing her platelets (clotting cells) and red blood cells (oxygen and energy carriers). This has made her dependent on platelet transfusions weekly and red blood cells transfusions roughly every month. We travel the hour each week to clinic in Providence and she gets her transfusions.
This has been the norm for us since 2012.

Today, the Rhode Island Blood Center had a special event to recruit new donors, especially for platelets. Along with the help of Dunkin Donuts incentives like gift cards and Patriots tickets, they are kicking off a goal of 1000 new donors this year. They asked my daughter and I to come and speak about how important it is for her to be able to receive platelets and how she is able to be a pretty normal kid and very active because of these wonderful donors. We also met a donor that is there to give platelets every two weeks and 3 people that were in the lab giving while we were there. This was a very special event to be part of and we were grateful to be included and to be able to thank these wonderful people who donate. The media was there and so we were on television too! Very cool to see my beautiful tween being her rock star self. Everyone at the blood bank already knew who she was and was excited to put a face with the name. They treated her like a real celebrity and it definitely has gone to her head!

Tons of friends contacted me to say they had seen us and our story. The people who have known us for a while and know us well, gave their thumbs up in one way or another. The people who haven't known us very long, seem to have a different reaction. People messaged that they feel bad for us or that our story left them heartbroken. They are missing the point…

Medicine has come far enough to have a process for giving your own blood to another person who needs it and then them being able to receive it and LIVE!! My daughter is able to be a competitive gymnast because she gets platelets. She is able to cheer for her school because she gets platelets. She is able to do sports because she gets platelets. She is able to LIVE because she gets blood!!

You need perspective in life. We could look at it like it sucks that we have to go to clinic each week. She misses a few hours of school on Thursdays and once every few weeks we have a really long day of transfusions and it's exhausting for us all. There is no protocol for her except keeping her stable. There is no definitive end to her treatment. But none of this is what's important. SHE IS ALIVE. She can get what she needs because of wonderful blood donors. She is able to spend as little time as possible at the clinic because of the amazing staff at
Hasbro Children's Hospital in Providence that treat us, and all their patients, like family. They know we have better places to be and much more fun things we'd rather be doing. While we are there, they have made it so

much fun that the kids sometimes don't want to leave! We have an amazing new group of friends who happen to be the strongest group of parents and kids you'll ever meet. We know this isn't the best situation. I live on faith. I've learned to live one day at a time and enjoy it as much as I possibly can and I'm teaching my kids to do the same. As we sit in clinic one day, and mostly one-half day, a week, there are plenty of people that have lost their children or other loved ones and they would do anything to trade places with us. Please don't ever feel bad for us. We have learned how important life is and how important it is to live each day fully. Don't pity us. My kids have a trampoline that makes our hematology team cringe, but YOU ONLY LIVE ONCE!! Don't be heartbroken in the least. We know how to have fun and live it up and we do!!

I don't know what the future holds. I do know that God is good. I do have a strong faith that my daughter will someday get better, hopefully in an "easy" way. I also know that we all need to keep our lives in perspective. While other children have limited life experiences and activities due to their conditions, my daughter is getting so many amazing opportunities to LIVE her life. She is getting to be mostly "normal" and, just like other tweens, drive me nuts. While other parents, including my own, have had to bury their children, my daughter is here and LIVING! I get to see her every day. I get to fight with her. I get to kiss her and tuck her in at night. I get to play her in air hockey. I get to watch her talk to boys and embarrass her. I GET TO BE HER

MOM!! So, please, please don't ever be heartbroken for us or pity us or feel bad for us. I get down sometimes myself, like we all do, but I know how blessed we are to be together as a family to love one another, to fight, to play, to hug, to cuddle, and to LIVE as amazing a life as we do.

Comp Mom~

I'm a competitive mom. Yup. I'll be the first to admit it. I'm competitive at heart. It probably stems from my mom and dad and growing up playing rummy, scrabble, cribbage, and anything else that brought on a little friendly competition. Okay, well we called it "friendly". When we won, we gloated. When we lost, we were teased. But it really all was in fun and it made me really enjoy the winning part, but still have fun either way. I also learned that I wasn't going to always win and that nobody would just let me either. I needed to practice and learn more to get better at whatever I wanted to win (btw…a lesson missed on all these kids today that get a trophy for participating!)

So, now I'm a mom and I still like to win. The thing is, I'm not JUST a mom. I'm a Sports mom. I'm a Sports mom that likes to see my kids do well, and yes, win. I have learned that getting better is important and I know full well that in the end we are only competing against ourselves. We should always strive to be better than we were yesterday in sports and in life. I see my kids compete. The boys are still young and looking at the sky or the grass while the ball is flying right at them. My girls, however, are outright, full-fledged, in the throws of competing. They go to practice and have fun with their friends and once in a while get frustrated, but, for the most part, they don't care. They do their thing. And that makes me happy for them. Seriously. I'm truly proud of them no matter the outcome, always. There's just that piece inside of me… that obnoxious, annoying piece…

They have a crazy mama at those comps that is a mess inside!!!! When one falls off the beam on her cartwheel or misses her second back handspring on her floor routine, I'm screaming inside.

When one misses something in the air or is a bit behind on a dance routine, I cringe. Right before the girls are about to compete, I'm sweating. My heart is racing. I might puke. I watch holding my breath. I'm a complete and utter idiot inside and I know it. I remind myself that neither of them is going to the Olympics. This is for fun and to stay active and they are both doing great. I get it, but my brain resists! It takes me time to unwind after watching a routine, no matter how they do! Yet, no matter what, they look happy as clams! I always say, "Great Job!" and high-five or give them a thumbs up from afar. Still, inside I want to scream!! If they do awesome, I want to jump up and down and run up and grab them and celebrate. If they miss something or fall, I want to squeeze them and comfort them assuming they must be crushed! Their nonchalant look drives me crazy! I know it's what we want. I know it's humble and good sportsmanship and, if they weren't like that, I'd probably need to have a talk with them. Still, drives a mom like me crazy! I can't be the only one like this…. surely, I can't. I know there are more like me, but you just won't admit it. Everyone wants to be nice, so damn nice. Well, admit it, like me. We can both be competitive and obnoxious and I'll still love you. Come over and see who wins at air hockey or rummy or scrabble. I'll still be your friend if you beat me…just as long as you bring the Xanax to my kids next competition.

Friends~

I notice sometimes people are surprised to know I still have very many friends from my childhood. I also make it a point to keep in touch with my friends and, in the midst of our busy lives, we do try to get together once in a while as well. The same way people are surprised that I've kept these friends for, in some cases, 35 years, I'm surprised that they have not. Now, friends in any capacity are great. I'm a true believer in surrounding yourself with good people. I also have made some wonderful friends at each different stage in my life, including the present. I have some amazing people I am blessed to call my friends that I have only known just a few years. I just still do not understand how some people don't keep in contact with their childhood friends.

In my case, I don't believe there are any people better equipped to know and understand and accept me than my childhood friends. They have seen me at my worst and at my best. They have seen my awkward stage...or years. They know what I look like with a mullet. They remember when I was fat. They remember me before the contact lenses. They still love me!

We know each other's entire families for better or worse. We still remember each other's phone numbers. We knew each other's pets. We drove in each other's cars. We were taken together on family vacations and crazy road trips. We were there for everyone's first kiss, first crush, first heartbreak, first school dance, graduations, proms, parties, and also for the first devastating losses.

Our parents were by default parents to each kid that walked into their house. They stuck by us and fed us and put up with all of our drama. Mom and Dad were Mom and Dad no matter who they belonged to. When my mom was diagnosed with leukemia and died 3 months later, my friends showed up at my door with mint chocolate chip ice cream and jimmies from

Friendly's. This is something I will never forget and always appreciate and love about them. Nothing could be said or done to bring my mom back, but these people did what we had always done to cheer each other up. What seems trite to some spoke volumes to me. We still know ice cream can make you feel even better than booze sometimes. Not a lot of people get that, but my best friends do.

As adults we have learned that life changes rather quickly and that it's not going to stop changing. Some changes are good and some changes are not. Old friends knew us before all these changes. They knew us at a time when we could just have fun without many of the stressors that we encounter as adults. Spending time with these friends takes me back to when things seemed so simple. And they were. I need my friends. I will always need my friends. They make me laugh and wipe my tears and remind me of who I really am under the stress that sometimes can overwhelm us all. They also remind me of my hopes and dreams and of who I want to be and of what I want to accomplish. They support me and they never judge me or my actions or my decisions. It's an unconditional love. It is a love like no other love and I am grateful to have this in my life.

Life Skills~

My seven-year-old cooks the best scrambled eggs I have ever eaten. This is not an exaggeration. He found a combination of herbs he adds to them to make them quite savory and they just melt in your mouth. Is he a prodigy? Is he a genius? Well, we are all a bit biased when it comes to our own children, so I do think he is perfect. However, the reason he can do this is because of one reason and one reason alone.

I let him try.

It's that simple. I've always encouraged my children to cook with me in any way they were able to at any given age. They all love to cook. I wasn't afraid of the messes they were going to make. I wasn't afraid of them messing something up or making it taste funny. I let them try. I let them do what they think is best when it comes to what they are cooking. We have had many messes and some disastrous outcomes that nobody wanted to eat. We have also had quite a few laughs about it and they have learned from their mistakes. Just as in all of life, we all need to make our own mistakes and do it better the next time. When my son was 3, he learned to crack an egg. By the time he was 5, he was making over easy eggs for himself every morning. He was taught how to use the stove. He knows safety because I taught him. He knows how to use a knife because I taught him. He tells us which burner he used so we all know which one is still hot. He let's his 3 year old brother mix things and gets him excited to help as well. His expertise has widened from just eggs. He makes a great chicken soup and some mean guacamole as well as a few other specialties. He's not the only one who has these skills. For years now, I'll smell something yummy when I wake up on a Saturday morning, walk downstairs, and my 11-year-old is taking a cake or some other concoction out of the oven. We are still working on the clean up part, but she certainly has become awesome at making things from scratch! My 10-year-old loves to decorate cakes and cupcakes. She enjoys making unique treats and made us some amazing whoopee pies not too long ago.

My friends have seen my kids cook and comment on how crazy it is that they do it at such a young age and without my help. Like I said, I let them try. Too many parents seem to do everything for their kids, as if their kids are going to break or somehow be too fragile to put in the effort themselves. We all need to let them try! And not just in the kitchen!

The world is so concerned with reading, math, science, social studies, technology, etc. I'm on my 7th year home schooling. I've taught my children all of those things, but I've also paid attention to life skills. My children know how to use the washer and dryer. They unload and load the dishwasher. They take out the trash. They sweep the floor. The older children help feed and dress the baby. I let them take off on their bikes around the neighborhood together. I love that they explore. They know the rules. They know about safety and emergencies. We are fortunate to know our neighbors.

Yes, my children have sat down and had to memorize facts and written out worksheets. But they also know how to count money back at a grocery store. They learned science and math and reading from cooking! I was so excited when my 10-year-old came home from school and told me that they were doing fractions and it was so easy. She said some other kids were having trouble, but she just remembered what she learned from measuring when we cook! I want my kids to be safe, so I teach them how. I want my kids to learn independence, so I give them some in an age-appropriate way. I want my kids to learn to be self sufficient, so they must help out around the house and practice life skills everyday. It is definitely not always pretty. Getting kids to do chores can really suck. I just persist. I don't back down. I don't give in. I talk to my kids about the importance of being a team. We all need to work together in order for our household to run smoothly. It not only helps them to learn and grow into responsible adults, but it helps me too!

Being single, I have met grown men who send their laundry out, who have their mommies clean their houses, who can't even boil water for pasta, and even men who are extremely book smart, but have no social skills! Meanwhile, my 2 middle kids are fighting over who gets to have the "magic wand" (aka Clorox toilet wand) to clean the toilets!

And to their future spouses I say, "YOUR WELCOME"!

Oxygen Mask~

I went away for one night over a weekend last year. It is the only time I have ever been away from my kids for an overnight. The next afternoon, in the kitchen, my 9-year-old said to me,
"Mom, why are you being so nice to us today?"
Wow. What a wake up call! And it should NOT have come as a surprise. You take a burnt out, 24/7 single mom of 4 and get her a night off and she comes back refreshed?!? Wow! What a revelation!

When we board a plane, before take-off, they always give us the oxygen mask speech. They always tell us to put our mask on before helping others, including our own children. If we don't, then we will pass out and not be any good to anyone! TAKING CARE OF OURSELVES IS LIKE PUTTING OUR MASKS ON FIRST!

Unfortunately, society gives out quite mixed messages. We hear how awesome it is that women can "do it all". They can work, take care of children, take care of a house, etc… Then we are told to make sure we are taking care of ourselves and being good to ourselves and taking some time out to do things we enjoy. Then there's the "mom guilt" that comes along with every single thing we do or say. Moms (and dads!), especially single ones with their kids all the time CANNOT do it all. WE CANNOT. Something's got to give. It seems that in most situations, it's us and our sanity and our mental and physical health! Why do we feel selfish when we do something that puts us first? What we are doing is becoming a better parent, friend, and person! We are teaching our children an important lesson in self-care.

I believe we need to put our oxygen masks on first! We are no good to our children if we don't! We are not being selfish! Think of all we do for our children! We have them in every activity we can find. We cart them across towns and states for sports. We make sure they are clothed and fed. We make sure they see their friends. We do this and laundry, dishes, floors, bills, and keeping cars and yards maintained! This is not all possible for one person to do! I decided something was going to give at my house and it can't be me. Laundry can wait. I can let my kids entertain themselves. I can get a babysitter. I need my time, my outlet. I need to take breaks. Call me selfish. I need to run. I need to workout. I need to go out with my friends and others I care about. My children are not going to break if they are left alone for an hour or two while I run or take an exercise class. Independent children are a good thing! They will be ok if they do not have me entertaining them. They will be ok if they are trusted to not kill one another because Mommy needs to get herself a little break. This morning I needed to run. I knew I needed to run. Every kid needed something from me. Every.Single.One. It took me 3 hours from when I woke up to get my ass out the door and run, but I did it. And it was all ok. I put myself…FIRST (gasp!) for 2 hours out of 24. Nothing bad happened! The only result is that I feel really good and got some stress out! I love my children, obviously, and I made sure they all had what they needed before I left. I'm so grateful, especially after losing loved ones, that we have each other. We are a very close family and that's a great thing. I'm still a 24/7 single mom though and that's a tough thing to be. I have learned to do things for myself and my sanity. At this point I can see the burn out and I'm barely keeping it at bay. I'm pretty sure I could use at least a week away to refresh my batteries, but ironically, I wouldn't do that because I certainly would miss those little shits too much to enjoy it! I would take one night again though in a heartbeat! According to my kids, I'll be a nicer mom for it!

Cloned~

As a Gemini, I have been told before that I fit the "multiple personalities" bill. I believe this is a good thing considering all of the hats that I need to wear on any given day to make life happen for my family and me. However, my son and I had a conversation about me being cloned. Now if that could happen, it would be way easier on my brain and my body! I might be able to think less and sleep more! The monkey banging the cymbals in my head could just finally take an effing break! Here are the clones we decided I need.

1. The Cleaning Clone

This clone would have the sole job of cleaning every room in the house, decluttering, and organizing on a regular basis. Most days, my house looks like a twister went through. Oh wait, it did! In the form of FOUR kids! We all know the drill. We clean one room spotless and feel so good about it and become excited about the time we will now have for other things. Then, we walk out of that room to see that, while we were cleaning there, the kids were pretty much shitting up the rest of the house. Now, I got to say it's great to hear people say, "Oh you just gotta keep on them!" BAHAHAHA!!! To them, I lift a huge middle finger and mentally give them a punch in the throat. You see, anyone that truly knows children, knows that it is a constant battle to get them to pick up! Some days are easier than others. Sometimes I just don't want to scream anymore! I feel like I spend 90% of my children's lives reminding them to pick up their shit! Its exhausting! Many times, no matter how clean or disgusting your house is, you need to just go to the playground or snuggle and watch a movie and let it all go to shit! This brings me to clone #2.

2. The Play Clone

OMG uninterrupted time with my children doing fun stuff and not thinking about anything else, but being there right then?!? Now THAT is an amazing feeling!

My Play Clone needs to take the kids to the movies, the bike path, kick a ball around outside, read more books on the hammock, and all the other things I really want to spend my whole day doing! They are only young once! I spend too much time feeling like I'm missing out on the fun stuff with them because of all the "other" stuff that needs to be done. This is the single most frustrating thing I would change if I could!

3. The Paperwork Clone

Bills, health insurance paperwork, permission slips…they all keep piling up! Just when I sit down for a couple of hours and make a dent, the mail comes! Lo and behold, there's more! It never ends! Taking care of the paperwork that goes into raising a family is nothing less than a full-time job in and of itself!

4. The Errand Clone

This chick would be hitting the post office, the bank, the dry cleaners, the grocery store, town hall, Target, Lowe's, and all the other places that are on my mile long to-do list of shit that I've been meaning to get to! If I get a chance in between home-schooling my son and cleaning to run any errands, the list is never completely finished before we are heading off to after school activities. I have things in the back of my car that I claimed I would drop off somewhere 7 months ago!

5. The Teacher Clone

I love home schooling. I was blessed to do it with my daughters for 6 years. I am now doing it with my son for 1st grade. The difference between then and now is.... drum roll please...all the fucking hats I wear! And know what? There are people out there that will read this and think,
"Gee, everyone is busy. It is what it is. Just deal with it or put him in school." Trust me, I have met these people. To them, I again shoot the middle finger. Guess what? If you are reading this and you are a single mom or dad

with multiple children and you are making it all work, then I am truly happy for you! However, I'm coming up on 2 years being widowed and I have NOT gotten my shit together yet. It is not from lack of trying either. I know I will get there. If you think you could be one of my clones, then by all means.... When it comes to my children, I want what's best for them. I believe home schooling is still best for my 1st grader for several reasons that would be another blog entry entirely! So...a teacher clone would be great. Watching our children learn and hit milestones like reading and mastering subtraction are truly exciting parts of my life!

6. The Chauffeur Clone

Luckily, I have a great dad who helps me carpool my kids where they need to be, but it would be awesome to just have a taxi waiting outside for their convenience! Gymnastics, cheerleading, football, faith formation, school, school activities, time with friends.... enough said.

7. The Writer Clone

I love writing! I need to squeeze time in at weird hours in order to get it done now. I need to do a little here and a little there. The thing about writing though is that, once you start and get on a roll, you don't want to stop! I will make it work with a little time here and a little time there because that's just how it needs to happen! Oh, but having hours at a time to write? Yes, I need this clone!

8. The Traveling Clone

I love to travel. Whether it be local or not, travel is the best form of education and memories that

I have ever experienced. I'm not just referring to vacationing in tropical places either. I want to see things I have never seen and meet new people from different cultures and learn about them. I want to give my children these experiences as well!

9. The Money-Making Clone

Well...duh?!? We can all use more, especially if I need to fund my traveling clone! Ha!

10. The Me-Time Clone

Working out, reading a book, going out for dinner, chatting with a friend over coffee, going to see a movie...these are all on my list of the things I enjoy that keep me semi sane. We all need some down time. I am a better person when I fit it in somewhere in my day or my week.

Each day, I juggle these jobs and more, just like we all do! I know I'm not alone. One of the reasons I write these entries is because I know others can relate. It makes me feel better when I read something and can say, "Yes! I know what you mean! ME TOO!" I hope someone reads

this and feels better knowing that life is crazy for all of us. I do believe we just need to do the best we can. Eventually, it all really does get done. I also believe that we need to remember what is important and count our blessings. I am guilty of doing something because I think it needs to be done that instant, instead of taking 10 minutes out to read with my kids and just take a break. I am working on this. I need to remind myself that the dishes in the sink don't matter, and neither do the crumbs on my floor. It matters that my kids laugh and know that I love them. It matters that I do what I know I need to be happy inside and take care of myself. So, I suppose
I would benefit if I had 10 of me, but, seeing as I'm pretty sure the world couldn't handle it, I will just continue to do the best I can. Multi-task on my friends, multi-task on....

Kels~

Online dating sucks. Okay, any dating sucks. Being on the other side of marriage just plain sucks! That dating world is full of liars, assholes, and people that view relationships as disposable. It's extremely frustrating to say the very least! However, it seems to be the only way to meet anyone these days! If you can't beat 'em, join em! So, I've decided that writing about it would definitely give others that "Me Too!" moment. If you're dating after 30 or 40 even, then I'm pretty sure you can relate to my experiences. Following is just one of many....

I stood outside the restaurant waiting for the man I had yet to meet who was supposed to be my date for dinner and assuming I was being stood up. Oh, how I wish I had. As a car peels down the street with a man hanging outside the driver's side window, I prayed. "Please no. Please please, please NO." The car whips into a parking spot, narrowly missing the car next to it.

A man, excuse me, a very, very tiny man jumps out the door and yells across the street at me, "Hey, Kels!". I tried not to make eye contact, like it wasn't me. My name surely could NOT be Kels? I looked around behind me, crossing fingers and toes that another woman, any other woman in the world was behind me. Nope. He came running up the restaurant stairs to me. This very tiny man said hello again. I politely said hello as I stepped back. It's amazing how different one can look in an online photograph. Just.Fucking.Amazing. Now, I would like to think that I am not vain. I have met people who are not as good looking as they seem because they have an awful personality and also men who are just ok and their personality makes them look way better. Either way, I don't like to be lied to. Bottom line. If your pictures show that you are jacked and have hair and look about 20 and your profile says you're 5'8", then you should NOT be looking me in the eye at a mere 5'2". You also should not have a comb over or weigh less than me. I'm sorry, but this is lying. If you will lie about how you look, what else will you lie about? I took a deep breath and tried to pull all the positive thoughts from deep in the abyss of my brain. I've already got a babysitter. I'm kid less for a few hours. The weather is nice. I can enjoy a meal out without being interrupted, therefore eating an entire meal while it is still hot. Okay, these were the positives... Well, I would rather cut up my kids' food and go to the bathroom 15 times and pull the boys apart from wrestling in the middle of the floor any.fucking.day. than be here now with this man. Ugh. I'm pretty sure he forgot his meds. He's all over the place. Hands flailing, talking so fast and loudly that I have no clue what he is telling me about. I nod and smile and order a drink. The drink comes and he just won't shut up. The food comes and I really have no appetite. If he calls me "Kels" one more time, I'm going to throw my chicken at him. I politely excuse myself to the bathroom. I call my Out right away. She gets it. This online shit is for the birds. You always need an Out, that one friend that will help you bail when you just can't take it anymore. I have my girl, my Out and she is ready to help. I sit back down to dinner and try to make small talk, but, honestly, this man doesn't even know what my voice sounds like.

However, the entire place knows he's there! Ugh. Double.Ugh. My phone rings! Oh HALLE-FUCKING-LUJAH!! What's that? Oh, no! I'm sorry, but my kid just won't stop crying. He needs me. Yes, I do understand that my sitter can probably handle him. (Asshole). But he must be sick and my kids always come first (THANK YOU GOD FOR THOSE LITTLE SHITS!) So, I must go. RIGHT.NOW. I'm so sorry. Yes! Of course, I was having a blast too! Yes, very, very disappointed. Oh, we will DEFINITELY (never) do this again! Here's some cash...Again, so sorry! GOTTA GO! Yup, sure call you tomorrow (as long as tomorrow is never)! Ok, bye!

…. Welcome to the world of dating….

An Open Letter to my Husband on the Anniversary of Your Passing~

Dear Bobby,

You've been gone 2 years today. Sometimes it feels like a dream. Sometimes it's still just so surreal. Sometimes it doesn't seem like any time has passed at all and other times it feels like a lifetime has gone by. When I think about it, it really is a completely different lifetime now.

First off, we miss you. The kids miss you. I talk about stories and fun times very often. I want them to always remember the fun. I know it wasn't all roses, but that's ok. I asked them to tell me what they think of first when they think of you. Joni said how you coached her in everything. Brody said he remembers when you went to so many different Dunkin Donuts because he wanted a strawberry frosted with sprinkles on a Saturday morning on Cape Cod in the summer and everyone was out, but you made sure you found him one! Hanna said she remembers you always wanting slush puppies and getting her them too, even though I would be mad. We tell the baby stories. I can't believe he was only 18 months when it happened. It's not fair. He will only know you through stories. That sucks. So, we do what we can to tell lots of stories and make sure there are lots of pictures of you for him to see. I miss you. Like I said, we had our problems, and it meant so much to me that we could talk about them and forgive everything in the end…but, we had so many good times too! You were my best friend. I miss when you sang me karaoke (I'm guessing the neighbors don't though). It was always either REO Speedwagon or Boys II Men. I love that I was able to meet someone who could let go and be crazy in the same way that I did. When we did stuff like that, we would roll our eyes at each other, but secretly loved it. Other anal-retentive people would never get our way of "crazy". I miss seeing you play with the kids, especially Brody. He needs that so badly. I try. I really do. I am just spread so thin. The boys have each other and play together a lot, but the baby beats on him and he knows he needs to be nice to his little brother. It gets old for him pretty quickly.

I miss being able to share milestones with you. The girls started school this year. I am so proud of them and how well they are doing. I know you would be too. When the girls got their first report card I cried. I just wanted to share that with you so badly. Brody has found this crazy love for football which makes me so happy! He loves to play center. Maddy is going to play this year too. He is so aggressive. I think he will have fun. I know you are there watching when they do everything, but it's not the same. I want to high five you. I want to hug you. I miss you.

I miss when you could make me laugh to cheer me up. I miss watching Storage Wars with you. I miss going to The Captain Kidd every year on our anniversary in July. I miss your stupid farmer's tan from surveying and how your neck was always red and you would swear you used sunscreen. I miss running with you. I remember that year at The Paul White Road race when we decided to compete with each other. I started out fast and was ahead of you until that last big hill before the finish line. You knew I suck at hills. Behind me I heard the Jaws shark music and I knew you caught me. You didn't go ahead though, and you could have easily done so. You ran the end with me and then made me go ahead of you into the chute so I would officially have won our little competition that day.

I miss the girls dressing up for the Father Daughter dance every year at the rec. I know they do too. I miss you telling everyone you would never forget our anniversary because it was the day the big fight broke out at the red sox game with A-Rod. I miss you. I remember the way you looked at me and cried when I was in labor with Hanna and you knew I was in so much pain. I remember you acting like the Red Sox won the world series in the ultrasound room when we found out Brody was a boy.

It has been so hard. The second year has easily been harder than the first too. In the first year, your head is spinning. In the first year, there is so much help too. After the first year, you start to settle into the crazy reality and everyone thinks you're okay now and the help and support starts to fade. But we aren't ok. I hate to admit it, but I can't do it all. I'm trying and it seems like there is always something that gets neglected and, sometimes, someone. I wear too many hats and it sucks. I really do enjoy being independent. I enjoy doing things on my own my way. There just is never enough time in the day or week or month for one person with four kids to get it all done. I am trying to take time for myself too. I know that's important. I go out with friends. I date. I thank God for my amazing girlfriends that put up with me. I wonder though if I will ever have a best friend like you again. I hope so. I know you want that for me.

Every season that goes by makes the kids and I miss different things all over again. Thank God I have the kids! They are awesome, even if they can be little shits. Oh, and the boys make sure I never miss a body next to me in my bed! They are awesome snugglers.

I know you are not in pain in any way now. I know you are happy. I know that you are watching us and guiding us and helping us. I know that you are with our son, Greyson. Give him lots of hugs and kisses from his mama. Give Gretzky a hug too. He was the best dog ever.

Tell my mom that this mommin' shit ain't easy and I am sorry that my room was always a mess and that I left dishes in the sink. Thank her too though for teaching me to cook and, especially her pumpkin bread. Thank her for helping to teach me how to be a good person and how to smile through tears. Have a brownie Sundae with Mike and tell him I miss his stinky farts. Tell my brother David that someday we will meet and thank you for always being my angel since the day I was born. Have some root beer with Uncle John and play some catch. I miss him being next door. Give them all hugs for me, seriously HUGE hugs. And I'm sending the biggest one I can muster up to heaven for you. Please continue to keep us safe and help us stay healthy and make Joni better. Please make year 3 easier than year 2. I know we will always miss you, but I have hope that everything in our lives will somehow get easier, that things just work out. I know they will. I love you. Thank you for being our angel.

Love, Your Best Friend, Kelly

Road Trip Lessons with My Kids...~

A few weeks ago, I began a journey around the country with my four kids. It has been many things: fun, exciting, educational, hilarious, frustrating, rewarding.... Here are some lessons I have learned.

1. After having 5 babies, I pee more than my kids. It is what it is. I cannot pee in a bottle while the car is moving since I'm the only driver. So, we stop. Often. Ugh.

2. Do not ask your 7-year-old son to help your 3-year-old son pee in a bottle when you are sitting in traffic. That will end with pee all over said 3-year old's pants.

3. Do not ask your 10-year-old daughter to help her 3-year-old brother pee in a bottle while sitting in traffic. She will try to hold his little wee wee in the bottle to avoid what happened when her 7-year-old brother tried

this before her. 3-year-old will think this is funny and shove her hand out of the way to allow his wee wee to fly around willy nilly. This will result in 3-year-old peeing on 10-year-olds face and shirt. 10-year-old will be very angry. Everybody else will laugh so hard that it's hard to breathe.

4.   People in the south are way nicer than Massholes. And yes, we are Massholes. Even when I think I'm being nice, compared to the southern people, I'm just a jerk.

5.   Do not empty a bottle of pee out the window while driving. It will blow back in and hit your children.

6.   Children should all be forced to pee and poop on the side of the road. You are not being gross, dirty, or classless. You are preparing them for college.

7.   If you don't drink soda and eat much fried food at home, don't do it on vacation. You will spend 2 days

walking around Disney World with the world's worst indigestion.

8. Sleeping in a queen-sized bed on vacation with 7- and 3-year-old boys is just as relaxing as it is at home....

9. When your children ask you some great questions about state facts and US history, you need to google. It has been 25 years since history class. The vague recollection I have of famous historical moments all blend together with decades of movies I've seen and rumors I may or may not have heard. It all comes back to you when you google, but sadly, in most cases, I am not smarter than a 5th grader.

10. You will never regret making memories. My trip sounded crazy to some people. Others claimed I was brave to drive through 18 places in 18 days by myself with my 4 kids. You only live once. Although at times I may be both, brave and crazy have nothing to do with it. We have ONE life to live and to love. My kids and I

will never forget this trip. Here's to many, many more insane adventures with my amazing (and sometimes crazy) family!

Speeding Through Life~

I drive too fast. I know I do. I see the speed limit sign says 50 and I do 60, 65 and I do 75. It has become how I roll. I don't have road rage. I don't cuss at people unless they are a real a-hole. I just have to be SOMEWHERE. ALL THE EFFING TIME. I have 4 kids and each one has their own schedule. I also have things I want or need to do as well. There are 24 hours in a day. There is no time to lose!

Raising a big family on my own requires an enormous amount of organization. Otherwise, it just doesn't run smoothly. We are NOT an organized family. We are loud. We fight. We can't find our shoes. Someone stole their sister's gym shorts. Someone needs to pee. The baby shit his pants on the way out the door. Someone forgot to eat breakfast. Someone has a 24-page notice from school that I NEED to read RIGHT NOW. Someone forgot they need a check for flute lessons. Someone only found one shin guard and there's practice today.

We have school, faith formation classes, gymnastics, soccer, football, music lessons, doctors appointments, swim lessons, homework, dinner, showers, etc. I could say "NO" to any of the "extracurricular" stuff, but I won't. My kids want to be active. They enjoy sports and trying new things. I do wish we had more downtime and I am always trying to figure out how to juggle and get it, but I still wouldn't say no. I love seeing them active and happy. I also know that this crazy, hectic schedule won't last forever.

I do wish my kids would be more cooperative and understanding. After one of them just took 16 minutes to find their right shoe, they will be in the car upset that we aren't going to be on time for something. They will ask me why I can't go even faster. They will request an exact number of minutes late we will be. Sometimes there are even tears. I remind them about 1000 times a week that I'm doing the best I can and that everything isn't always going to work out and be perfect. That's life. It is what it is. Inevitably, I feel "mom guilt". I tell myself we will be on time next time. Then, the next time, when we arrive 5 minutes late, I'm cursing and mad that it has happened again.

It seems that even when we leave early and it looks like we will make it somewhere on time, for some reason like a traffic jam or a school bus, we either just make it or are late again. We are teased by some friends because they know we will be late more than not. Many of my friends run late as well, which makes me way less stressed. I love inviting them over for dinner knowing that when the food still has 40 minutes in the oven, I will see their text about being 40 minutes late.

I wonder if there will ever come a time when we are on time for everything. I wonder if I should throw in the towel, but it's just not my style. I know I'm doing the best I can. I want to do it all and I want my kids to do it all. I cram too much into each day. I know I do, but I have great intentions and a good heart. We are completely unorganized, but I am working little by little to change that too. Rome wasn't built in a day, right? I have decided to continue to do the best I can at any given time. We all need to remember this in our lives. We are human. We mess up. We need to be easier on each other and ourselves! Remember, there will always be critics. Try not to be one of those. We are all here doing the best we can!

So, if you invite us to your party, please remember reheating food doesn't bother us in the least and, if we pass you on the highway, just wave and smile. A thumbs up wouldn't hurt either.

Small Town~

I didn't grow up in a small town. I grew up in a city, population 56,843. I did spend summers in a small town though. It's a beautiful town right on the water where the tourists quadruple the population of about 31,000 every summer. I was blessed enough to move to that small town full time in 2002. When I got here, all my summer friends had gone home for the winter and I pretty much didn't know anyone. The first thing my husband and I did was to join the local track club. They welcomed us warmly with wide open arms. They were some of the most wonderful people

I've ever met in my life. They quickly became friends and made my transition to year-round living in this small coastal town much, much easier. Since then, four children have made life a bit busy and I'm not involved much with the track club anymore. I still run, of course, but now it's when I can fit it in between gymnastics and soccer and swimming class and football and school. The one thing that sticks out in my head is how loving that group really was to me, and still are today. Over the years, I have realized that group is a true representation of this small town. This truly is a community with wide open arms.

For my first 26 years, I lived in a wonderful city as well. Now that I've spent some time in a good-sized city and a small town, I think I can honestly compare the two.

I never heard any negative comments about where I grew up until probably high school. By then, we were playing sports against other schools and going to multiple district student council functions where we were interacting with other kids from different towns and cities in our state.
I started to realize that our city, where I always felt safe, had this reputation for being "tough".

For years, I sort of "went with it" somehow thinking that this chubby band chick with acne was now badass. When I went away to college, my roommate was from another, much smaller town in my state about an hour from where I lived. She looked at me like I was a thug and must have guns and drugs. Again, I got a kick out of it because…well, she was prissy as hell and I really couldn't stand her!

When I moved year-round to my forever place here by the sea, I noticed I was still hearing much of the same negativity about my city of origin. Now, it was coming from adults. These adults were supposed to be well-educated people, yet still they believed the stereotypes and rumors, even having never stepped foot in my "big" city at any point in their lives. It started to make me defensive. I loved and still love that city. My memories of growing up include amazing teachers, hanging out at The Girl's Club after school making arts and crafts, the science fairs, taking pride in having the best softball teams in the state, playing outside with the neighborhood kids, marching in parades, and parents that were involved in the community in whatever ways possible. I was taught to get involved. I had friends from every background, every color, different beliefs and I was actually taught that this was ok. No, it was more than ok. This was GREAT. This was a representation of life! It didn't matter how much money we had or how much money they had. It didn't matter what side of the tracks (literally) you were from. I look back and feel that I grew up in a community that cared and still does care today. We helped one another. We stuck together. Somebody always had your back. I still have my roots there and I wouldn't change that for the world. When my husband was diagnosed with stage 4 stomach cancer and our childhood friends found out, they quickly helped in any way they could. Our awesome friends used their band to have a concert and get the community together for a giant fundraiser. They blew us away with their generosity of time, effort, and raising of money that truly helped my family more than they will ever know. I don't even live there anymore, but I'm still supported through an amazing network of great people! Today, some of my friends are teachers there, some are police officers and firefighters, and some are running that city. I take pride in seeing how they make a wonderful city even better every day. It is the same way I feel about where I live. This small town has already had my back on more than one occasion. This is a place where parents, teachers, police officers, firefighters, business owners, municipal workers, coaches, and residents from the North side to the East side all care about this town and the people in it. I see it where ever I go, and I'm proud.

When I had my fourth child stillborn and came home from the hospital feeling lost and overwhelmed, I was taken care of by this community. Two different churches had members going out of their way for my family. Strangers were doing my laundry to help us. Those strangers became friends. I felt supported by more than just my family. I saw a town come together for one of its own and fill a need. While my husband fought for his life, and shortly passed away 7 months later, this community came out full force in a way I never could have imagined. People helped me in every possible avenue. I felt loved and supported and humbled.

I mostly felt, and still feel, blessed.

A little over a week ago, NBC aired a special segment on my small town. It was highlighting one of our elementary schools and the way they have responded to help children in our community who have either lost a parent to drug overdose or are struggling with a parent with an addiction. It also showed what they are doing to help keep children away from drugs and give them avenues to talk to trusted adults and relieve their stress in productive ways. When I watched the segment, I was filled with pride. Again, I saw a community seeing a problem here and working above and beyond to fix it. So much so, in fact, that NBC came and spread this story to the rest of the country to use our town as an example of doing good for others and as a model other cities and towns can use for their own communities!

The next day, I was appalled when I scrolled down my Facebook feed. I was pretty sure we had all watched the same segment. However, I read comments that focused on the towns drug problem. Some even going so far as to say they were glad they had gotten out of here when they did and that the town wasn't like when they were a kid. I was seriously dumbfounded. I'm not sure what rock these people have crawled out from under, but let me enlighten you. DRUGS ARE EVERYWHERE!!!!! If you think for one second that your town or city is somehow immune from drug addiction, you are so very wrong. You know people addicted to drugs or that have overcome addiction. Trust me, you do. They are your neighbors, your co-workers. Some have made it and some have not. Some are buried in the cemetery next to your grandmother. This is happening everywhere!! To act like our town has more of a problem than every other place in our country is pure ignorance, completely missing the point, and just plain WRONG.

I'm proud of NBC coming out here. I'm proud to open my eyes at the world around me and see the good. This isn't a gift. This is making a choice to be positive in a world where we are bombarded by the media with negative. So much so, perhaps, that when a good, positive story comes out, some people can't even recognize it anymore?!?

I grew up in a place where there were most definitely drugs, crime, and people who just did bad things, but there was also a sense of community. There were good things happening every day. There were teachers walking kids home from school if parents couldn't. There were sports teams celebrating their wins at Friendly's, there were people helping at the shelter and food pantry. There were programs and activities everywhere to help the community and the people in it and to come together for our neighbors in need. This is exactly how I see the town I live in as well. In fact, look around you. This is every town and city "from sea to shining sea". This is our country, our amazing, wonderful country. This is where, yes, bad does happen, but so does good. There are copycat crimes. BUT there are also copycat solutions, fundraisers, and good deeds! The good can spread, IF we choose to focus on it! Look around where you live. Really look. Think about what you want to spread in your own community. You are a catalyst. Each one of us spreads something, positive or negative, whenever we speak or perform an action.

Open your eyes to the world around you. What do YOU choose to see?

Dad~

My dad passed away this week. He was 78 years young. Even though you see someone you love in poor health, and even though you know they will soon not be here, it still hits like a throat punch. Takes my breath away to think about it. I was blessed and need to share what I wrote to honor his memory.

Everyone who knew my dad, knew he was special. I've gotten messages and phone calls left and right about what an amazing, kind, generous, great man my dad was. Thank you so much for that! Our family has been through a tremendous amount of loss, some before I was even born. My dad was my backbone and the backbone of our family through it all. He has been my source for laughs and support and hugs and venting for my entire life. He truly was, and always will be, my best friend. Thinking about days without him makes me choke. So, I don't. I know he is another angel and will always be with me and with all of my children. I cannot get too sad. That wasn't my dad. It wasn't what he wanted. I want us all to remember him and smile. Here are some best thoughts and memories I personally have and also some from his family and friends that I wanted to share.

I happened to ask 3 people in a row…2 cousins and a friend what sticks out when they think of my dad. All of them said, "The Grand National and how damn fast he drove!" He loved that car! I remember he got it because it was one of the fastest cars in the nation. That fact was so lost on me, but not on my guy friends at Taunton High School. Whenever my dad let me take his car, I would be bombarded with pleading from them begging to get a chance to drive it. I am proud to say that I never let them! My dad would have killed me and that car would surely have been done in the hands of a teenage boy!

My dad gave us our first taste of a global education. As president of the Taunton Rotary Club, he brought Up With People to Taunton. We got to meet people from all over the world. This gave us a desire to learn more about other places and people and ways of life. He was in charge of several exchange programs throughout the years as well. Through these exchanges, I still have some wonderful friends. Thanks to him and my mom both, we were taught that we are part of a community larger than ourselves. We were taught to be understanding, non judgmental, and kind. My father truly did treat the janitor the same as the CEO. At the furniture store, I have been told, that when you walked in there and couldn't afford what you needed, you still took it home with the promise that you would come back each week and pay a little down. Many people have told me that it was the only way they ever would have been able to afford their first new bedroom or dining room sets. That was a special thing, that trust and faith that my father always kept in people.

My dad loved music and all kinds. He took me to my first concert. I was in 7th grade and got to see Bon Jovi and Skid Row! He took my friends and I to see SO MANY CONCERTS. Pretty sure he saw New Kids on The Block at least a dozen times…. not sure it was really his favorite singing group though. Years later, he was the chauffeur for my kids for school and activities. I always felt bad asking him to bring them somewhere or to pick them up, but he would insist. I soon learned that he loved that time together with them and so did they. My dad was way cooler than me, letting them listen to whatever they wanted on the radio. Eventually, their music grew on him and he ended up sometimes telling me I should be listening myself! My kids tell me that's one thing they will remember the most. Those car rides. He would spoil them with Starbucks or Dunkin or whatever else they asked for, and they knew I would have said no. My kids' friends all knew Pubby well too. He picked them all up at one time or another and he was always likely to be at the house when friends were over. He loved people. He took care of his friends, then my friends, and then was doing the best he could to take care of his grandkid's friends too. That's just the kind of man he was.

He was also patient. He let my friends and I get away with just about anything we wanted. He had plenty of times that he could have told them all to go home, but instead, he was more likely the one pulling out the deck of cards. And sometimes he would let us do things and get away with them as long as we promised not to tell my mother.

Speaking of Joan… A few weeks ago, my dad and I talked about him dying. It did break my heart. But I held his hand and I told him that it will never be okay for him to pass away because I want to hold onto him forever, but he had his brother, his 2 boys, and one heck of a gorgeous woman waiting for him. I told him that when the moment came for that reunion, I was sure I'd be seeing fireworks in the sky.

I love hearing all the wonderful things that people are telling me about him. I love that people have told me that they feel lucky and blessed to have known such a man. I am the lucky one though. That's my dad you are talking about and I got to have him for 41 years! It is too hard to say goodbye, but I know I don't have to. I know he isn't gone. I know that he is another angel. I know his helping days are not gone either. He will always be my best friend. Even though I already miss calling him 100 times a day or him calling me, I know he will still make sure that I know he is here. Death cannot stop the love between two people, nor will it make me sad for long. He has left a legacy for certain. And that legacy is truly filled with nothing but joy and kindness to the world around us.

I Love it When…~

My kids are givers. Total givers. Yours are too, right? These sweet little cherubs just do the sweetest things to test Mommy's limits, to see just how close I can get too crazy. Here is a short list of some of the things they do that I just love…

1. Never flushing the toilet. We have two bathrooms. Every single time I need to pee or shower or I'm just putting some towels away, I get to flush a toilet! I know how much fun it is to push that little handle. My kids are sweet to think of me and let me always be the one who gets a turn! Sometimes I even get to smell it and need to spray the button on the air freshener! I just love buttons! I especially love when they have all gone over and over again and left it for me, like a big fluffy nest of toilet paper. It's like staring at the big, beautiful sky filled with soft clouds, except on a blanket of shit instead of sky. So sweet. Oh! And don't forget, that's when it usually gets clogged too! I LOVE working a

plunger and I have become SO good at it. I need to remember to add that to my resume now that I think about it.

2.   Food in the sink. We have no garbage disposal. I love how my kids make sure they always leave a little something (or a lot) on their plates, especially since it is nearly impossible for me to get to the dishes every day. I believe they are so concerned about the mice and ants and fruit flies, seeing as they were an issue this past year. I apparently have been inhumane in trying to kill them or make them stop coming. Much nicer to feed them and all live in harmony! When I do get to the dishes, my kids know I always enjoy a good challenge. I love the caked-on food. That makes scrubbing fun. Oh, and that time I paid a plumber nearly 300 bucks because the tub and the kitchen sink were clogged and it all needed to be snaked and he showed me 16 plastic straws that had somehow gone down the kitchen sink drain…well that was super fun!!!!! Who knew disposable straws cost so much?? What a treat though

for the kids and I to learn about recycling in such a nice way. Yes, I love my givers...

3.   Laundry. Not sure if your kids are as sweet as mine, but my kids do know how much I love exercise. They make sure to put their dirty clothes right NEXT TO the laundry bins on the floor.

This way I always need to bend and reach to pick them up! I have been working on my bikini bod for the summer. So sweet!! Oh, and when I have no towel after a shower, but there are 13 dirty ones on my daughter's bedroom floor, well that's just perfect! I heard that air drying is much better for the skin anyways. Or if I manage to find and use a face cloth and it's nice and wet afterwards, I could just reuse it to wash the baby's face and really be saving the environment in just so many ways! My children really do care about nature.

4.   My girls "borrow" my things. Who doesn't LOVE running late and looking for their hairbrush, but not finding it ANYWHERE because their 12-year-old

put it in her backpack and took it to school? Come on now! You know you all raised your hands! The other day it was a total treat when I walked around the house for 10 minutes with no pants on because the same 12-year-old was wearing the ones I was looking for and wouldn't answer when I asked if anyone had seen them. She knows I just love a good mystery!

5. Leaving trash all over the house. If I ever need to wear an orange vest and carry a stick, I will have that shit mastered! Under the couch is the best. I mean, since you don't really look there every single day, that stuff can really add up and fester. It can be an entire hour of community service practice! Oh, and again, I love when the trash is on the floor right next to the trash can. Mama's workin' those abs, baby!

These kids really do care about my health. All this extra exercise will really pay off. I love how they give me all these extra reasons to sweat! Just wait 'til you see me on the beach this summer! We will be the family with no towels, surrounded by trash, and leaving all the food around for the sweet, beautiful seagulls that we all just love so much!

Homesick~

Mostly I like to write with humor. I seem to find humor in nearly every situation and I think that's definitely a good thing. There are some situations where it is harder than others. This entry is not one of the funny ones. It's just some real life. I am not writing this for pity. Those who know me well know that it is not my style. I am very much someone who tries to always pull myself up and out of life's bullshit and move on with hope. I am doing that every. single. day. I think I feel the need to write this entry more for understanding. I am not even sure that others will really, truly understand and it doesn't really matter. I guess maybe it would just get it off of my chest or be "part of the healing process". I think we all have situations that hit us and, if we are to be successful human beings, we need to heal in whatever form that may take.

I lost my dad 3 months ago. Writing this made me think about how long it has been. It's shocking to me that its been 3 months. It seems more like 3 weeks maybe. Besides my kids, he was what I had left. Now, I do NOT discount my amazing friends in the least and they know that. I love them and they help me and get me through each day with sometimes venting and sometimes, most times, laughter. But not having immediate family is hard. That's just a fact. I lost my mom when I was 25. I felt so lost. Your parents are responsible for your identity. You rely on them for so much, at least in my case I did. I know I am lucky for all that I did have with my mom, but greedily, obviously, I wish I had more. She wasn't there when I got married or had babies. That was hard. But, guess who was there? My dad. And guess who amazingly did all he could to comfort me, help with baby advice, and listen to me, and make me smile? My dad.

Two years after my mom died, my brother passed away. He was 4 years older than me and, after growing up with the normal sibling rivalries, we were just starting to become friends. Losing him came so soon after losing my mom, that I'm still not sure I ever grieved properly (as if there is a proper way!). My dad and I had each other. I am sure that for him losing a son was gut wrenching and much harder than losing a sibling, no matter how much it hurt me. He was still my dad and he was still there to pick up the pieces and give me strength and hope.

Almost 3 years ago, I lost my husband to cancer, leaving me to raise 4 young children on my own including the youngest at only 18 months old. And guess who was there for me? My dad. In every way, shape, and form that man was there for me. He did more than I could ever have asked for me and my kids. The relationship he had with my children was untouchable, just so damn special. It was almost as special as the relationship he had with me. My dad was my sounding board, my comedian, my biggest cheerleader, my confidant, sometimes my punching bag, and always my best friend. I always felt that all would be ok. He made it so. He gave me hope and brought peace to my crazy, single mom life. He drove my kids to activities so I could cook us all dinner. He brought them to school in the morning so I didn't have to wake the baby. He called me a million times a day or I called him. It was just normal. Every time the kids said something cute, I called him. When they pissed me off, I called him. He went around my house and if something were wrong and he couldn't fix it, he would call someone who could before I could blink. He saw problems before I knew there could be a problem and he would make sure there wasn't. As his health deteriorated, I watched carefully when he played with the kids, taking pictures in my head, knowing it wouldn't last forever. It truly is amazing how much this man spoiled me, but I always knew he was a generous, amazing man and I would like to think that I never took that for granted. Through all of my losses, our losses, I had him. We had each other. Even the times I felt lonely after losing my husband, I was never truly alone because I knew I still had my dad. Then he passed away. I had felt this feeling before and it bugged me that I couldn't pinpoint exactly what I have felt.

Then, I figured it out.

Have you ever been away from home? I don't mean on vacation either. I mean college, boot camp, or moving to another state? In 1996, I went away from home to Colorado for Up With People. That was the longest amount of time I would face away from my family and friends and what I knew as familiar. It was this lost, lonely feeling. It was true homesickness. Being homesick then was hard, but I could call home and I knew I would get visits from my family and that I would return home. I had that longing for them, that feeling in the pit of my stomach. I just wanted to hug them and not let go and they were miles and states away. It made my heart break at times, but I would pick up the phone and hear their voices and I would start counting down until their next visit or my days back home. It would be ok. I would hug them again, see them, hear their voices. That empty feeling, that horrible feeling of homesick in the pit of your stomach, that's what I've got now. Only now, I can never "go back home". The only visits are through pictures, stories, dreams, and my medium friends. That homesickness is something I know I need to learn to live with and I know I will. I am too strong not to. I have my mom and dad in me. I have 4 amazing kids. I do truly love life. I know I am blessed. This all gets me through, but it will take time.

I am also now left with truly raising 4 kids as a single mom. My dad never left me feeling that way. Like I said, he spoiled me. I am at a point in my life where 4 kids need my attention, my house needs my attention, the cars need my attention, my father's estate needs my attention, bills need my attention, cleaning out two houses needs my attention, trying to get back out into the work world to better my family's financial situation and for my sanity needs my attention, taking online courses needs my attention, carving out time to take a breath needs my attention. I am wearing too many hats for one person and I know it. Not sure others realize this and that doesn't matter to me, as long as they don't ask me to do something and wonder why it takes me so long to get to it. I am spent. I am lonely. My head is spinning. My world is upside down. And, most of all, I miss my dad with all my heart.

So, if I don't seem like myself lately, please remember this isn't the usual me. This isn't who I want to be and I won't stay here and I am not wallowing. It's just a lot and I need time. I am chipping away, I know that. I will be me again, and soon. I am sure of it. In fact, like every time I have come out of the storm, I have hope that I will be an even better version of myself. If I can help anyone have hope in their own struggles, then mine have been blessings.

3 years~

A Letter to Bobby from this side of the clouds.

Dear Bobby,

Thursday, the 17th of May, it will be 3 years since you've been gone. That thought has caused this horrible choking feeling in me, as it always does a week or 2 before your anniversary. I've been thinking a lot these past few months of "our song". "Bent" by Matchbox Twenty probably seems strange to most people, but it was perfect then and still is now.

"If I fall along the way, pick me up and dust me off. And if I get too tired to make it, be my breath so I can walk."

A lot of falling and picking up was done in our marriage over the years, as is the case with marriage. Since you got too tired to make it, I have been your breath here on

Earth. I give my life to our four gorgeous children and through them, you still walk. We tell stories and look at pictures and make sure that you are remembered, that you live on.

I'm not going to lie and say it's been easy. In fact, I'm falling along the way sometimes and I need you to pick me up and dust me off in whatever way you can from heaven. I don't ever want to become jaded like the song says. I know life is too good and so are people. Our kids need to know how great life and this world are, and I need to be the one to show them.

I remember saying that year two without you was harder than year one. Year one was filled with shock and loads of help and understanding from people. Year two most people think the worst is over and you must be ok, so they aren't around as much to help. They don't realize this is when you truly are feeling thrown to the wolves. Trying to adjust still to doing it all and being it all for the kids is a big job. I'm proud of how we are all doing. I'm proud of myself. But it's still hard. I guess the third year without you has been extra tough because we lost my dad. The kids really relied on him, even more than ever since you've been gone. And so did I. But this past year has been filled with some great things and amazing memories too.

Last summer I decided to use some of our memorial fund to create a memory the kids and I would never forget. I packed them up in the Suburban and we took off for a road trip: 4000 miles and 18 states in 18 days, just the kids and me. And why the heck not? We only have this one life and I am damn well certain to make it a great one! Our kids have now seen 25 out of 50 states! I think that's pretty cool.

Maddy is 4 now. He is a stubborn little bugger, just like a male version of Hanna. He wants to do everything himself. He just learned to ride his bike without training wheels so he can be like the big kids! He only eats chicken fingers and mac n cheese. He loves to workout with his mama. Oh, and he climbs in bed with me usually right before the sun comes up and snuggles me then falls back asleep. I love that. Reminds me of how blessed we truly are!

Brody still misses the heck out of you on a regular basis. He needs positive male role models in his life. We have been blessed with some amazing men as football coaches for him. I am so grateful for that. We also have made wonderful friends through school that have been nothing less than a Godsend. This summer Brody will get to go fishing finally more than we have been able to. He absolutely loves fishing. He tells me he knows you are there when we fish. He went to school this year and I couldn't be prouder. He has awesome friends and he is really becoming a responsible young man.

Hanna is still as emotional and feisty as they come. She has a mind of her own as always. She is a force to be reckoned with, our little Hurricane Hanna. She decided she loves to run with me. It makes me so happy. It's such a challenge to find time to spend alone with each child and they need it. This gives her and I an opportunity to have that time. She did gymnastics this year. She did awesome. I love how flexible she is and how she wants to try so many different things. She is so unique. She is a wonderful artist too! We have really discovered that this year. Very cool to see someone inherit my parents' great talent!

Joni is 13 next month. Need I say more? I love that kid more than she will ever know, but boy does she push buttons! She played soccer and basketball this year and loved them both. She loves sports and her friends. She has definitely been blessed; her best friends are a true gift from
God. I couldn't ask for better kids to be hanging around our house. I have a blast when they are all over. She is also becoming more gorgeous than ever and starting to fit into my clothes and shoes. I'm not sure whether or not this is good. I mean, if she fits in mine, I could technically fit in hers?

I feel overwhelmed and like a hot mess most days. I fly by the seat of my pants. I do the best I can and try to cut myself slack, but those that know me well know I am pretty hard on myself. I started teaching Pound. Best. Thing. Ever. I get to hit and it's legal! I love bringing it to others.

We all need a good stress release.

I know that I am "bent" right now. I'm sure that I always will be in some way. We all are. But unlike the song, I know that my pieces will be put back together again. As my favorite line in the song says, "when my smile gets old and faded, wait around I'll smile again."

We miss you RPG. A whole lot.

Beach Days~

I LOVE beach days. I always have, my entire life. All I've ever needed to make me happy was some sun, salt, and sand. I remember it being the simplest pleasures, those days at the beach. As this summer comes to a close, I'm reflecting on my summer days versus those of my children.

We bring a lot of crap to the beach. 13 beach chairs, 23 different bags of snacks, 9 inflatables, 15 noodles, 43 towels (that I'm going to be the one to wash), and 652 juice boxes. First of all, the chairs mostly do not get used, but the one day I just bring my own, every kid will scream and fight over sitting in mine and whine incessantly about why I didn't bring their chairs too. I bring plain potato chips, bbq chips, dill pickle chips, popcorn, Cheetos, and tortilla chips. Know what happens? Someone asks why I didn't bring the pretzels. Every. Single. Time. I bring water, fruit punch, pink lemonade, and grape juice. Someone wants the apple juice! I remember jumping on my bike and wrapping my towel around my shoulders when I was a kid! That's all I needed! When I was hungry, I rode my ass home and got myself a fluffernutter and went back down. I wonder if my own children would implode if I tried this with them? I have implemented the "you want it, you carry it rule". That has led to none of them wanting anything. So, I pack as much as I can fit on the old stroller (my own ghetto version of a beach buggy) and I roll it down to the beach. I do all the work except for carry their whining little bodies. I grab the football, soccer ball, volleyball, and floating ball. When we get to the beach, they whine that they have nothing to do!

Ah, yes… there's another thing! These poor, deprived children that spend nearly every summer day on the beach have nothing to do! Perhaps some kid land locked in Nebraska would want to trade places with these kids?!? Complaining about going to the beach, as far as I'm concerned, is as stupid as complaining that you have too much money or that the portion size at a restaurant is too huge! Come the eff on now! Seriously!

Next time I'm over at the cabana bar having a drink, I'm going to complain that the mudslide is just too good. Oh, and the sand is too soft on my feet. The shirtless men are too good looking. My friends are too nice. Yada yada yada…

I'll start tomorrow, on Labor Day, putting out a large jar on the table for my ungrateful kids and their ungrateful friends. Whenever they complain or whine, they need to put money in the jar. Next summer, I'll use it to buy peanut butter, fluff, and bread and spend the rest on my mudslides.

Siblings~

I was blessed to grow up with my brother. He was about 4 years older than me. He teased me. He punched me to get the remote control or the last devil dog. His friends stole my food too, sitting on me and making me watch them eat the sandwich I had just made. He was loud. When it was the two of us and my parents, I couldn't get a word in no matter how hard I tried. He would sit and read the magazines with cars for sale and make us all listen. That annoyed the crap out of me. I remember when he shut the door of the Dodge Caravan on my fingers. It was definitely a joy to have him as my brother. It was a joy because this is the stuff that siblings do to each other! They also teach us. Having Mike as my older brother taught me how to get along with others, no matter how they treated me. It taught me how to stand up for myself. It taught me that, even when you know you did nothing wrong, someone will probably always think you did. It taught me that there was someone looking out for me even when I didn't know it.

Next time I'm over at the cabana bar having a drink, I'm going to complain that the mudslide is just too good. Oh, and the sand is too soft on my feet. The shirtless men are too good looking. My friends are too nice. Yada yada yada...

I'll start tomorrow, on Labor Day, putting out a large jar on the table for my ungrateful kids and their ungrateful friends. Whenever they complain or whine, they need to put money in the jar. Next summer, I'll use it to buy peanut butter, fluff, and bread and spend the rest on my mudslides.

Siblings~

I was blessed to grow up with my brother. He was about 4 years older than me. He teased me. He punched me to get the remote control or the last devil dog. His friends stole my food too, sitting on me and making me watch them eat the sandwich I had just made. He was loud. When it was the two of us and my parents, I couldn't get a word in no matter how hard I tried. He would sit and read the magazines with cars for sale and make us all listen. That annoyed the crap out of me. I remember when he shut the door of the Dodge Caravan on my fingers. It was definitely a joy to have him as my brother. It was a joy because this is the stuff that siblings do to each other! They also teach us. Having Mike as my older brother taught me how to get along with others, no matter how they treated me. It taught me how to stand up for myself. It taught me that, even when you know you did nothing wrong, someone will probably always think you did. It taught me that there was someone looking out for me even when I didn't know it.

It taught me that you can fight with someone and still love them more than anything in the world. My brother was taken too early. He was only with us for 31 years. In that time, he left his mark. That's for sure. He was kind, smart, handsome, generous, and above all else funny as heck.

Tonight, I heard my girls upstairs making way too much noise considering that their brothers were sleeping. At first, I asked them to quiet down. Then, I let it go. I let it go and listened. I listened to the silly giggles that turned into outright snorting. I thought about how precious it is to have a sibling, right there with you, laughing with you, sharing a joke, a bond. Those girls fight SO MUCH. They also laugh. They get along. They are best friends. I am pretty certain they don't yet know that they are each other's best friend, but someday I have hope they will. I cherish every stupid memory I have of my brother.

31 years goes by in flash. The time that he has been gone seems like a whole different lifetime. I may have gotten cut short on the sibling stuff, but I now get to see

my 4 children fight like crazy, but then also know EXACTLY how to make each other laugh. That's definitely the good stuff. Cherish that my friends, cherish that.

Is That a Donut? ~

Today I really didn't do anything on my to do list. I am always going at a constant pace. If it seems like I never stop, it's because I don't. Even on the weekends, we don't always just relax. Last weekend I decided to treat myself. By treating myself, I mean that I decided to clean MY bedroom. The toys scattered around my dresser do not belong to me. The overflowing baskets of laundry are not just my clothing. The 7 water bottles half full on my night stand are not mine.
So, yes, this was a real treat for Mom. I don't eat in my bedroom, yet the vacuum sucked up a moldy ear of corn and what I think was a half eaten donut.

So, today, I slacked.

I remember when I used to walk into the house and sit down. I would take a break and watch a little TV. Now, I need to do laundry, get dinner ready, or any number of other tasks. My children do help with chores, but, for the most part, it's all on me. I spend quite a bit of time driving my children wherever they want to go as well. I bring them to soccer, football, hip-hop dance class, school activities, friends houses, and every place in between. On any given day if someone asks me what I have planned, there is usually an extremely long list. I rarely get to everything on the list, but I don't stop until it's bedtime. I know this isn't good, but I do it anyway. I hate to procrastinate. I hate to know that there are things that I should be doing. Over the last several months, life has been pretty upside down. Just when I thought I had a handle on raising four kids on my own after their dad died, we had another rug pulled out from underneath us when my dad died. Life has definitely been an adjustment again! I spent months cleaning out my father's house. Thank God for the friends who helped me with that! It still took an emotional toll. I finally got rid of his car. I sold furniture of his and threw a lot of things away.

I sold his house. Perhaps it's just hitting me that I've experienced that closure. Perhaps it's the nasty rain that this day brought. But I am tired. I am not just physically tired, but emotionally and mentally drained. So, today I did not check things off my to-do list. Today, after I played with the preschoolers at my son's school and then taught my pound class at the gym, I slacked off. I hate to admit it, but I did. Before I went to the gym, I had plans to run 2 miles and do some extra ab work after my pound class. After all, two weeks ago I committed to losing the 20 pounds I gained over the last 3 years. I've already lost five and been really working hard for that accomplishment. When I left the gym, I still had plans in my head to go home and run on my treadmill and do that ab work. I decided to stop for a coffee. Next door to the coffee shop is a new, cute, little boutique. It is filled with unique gifts. It's a place that I wanted to check out for a couple of months. I decided to take a look. I didn't buy anything, but it was nice to take a breath, stop, and just take my time. Then I grabbed my coffee and headed back home. When I got home, I chatted a little bit with my daughters. They are now back to homeschooling. (So, yeah, that's been an adjustment as well.) I treated myself to sitting down and eating lunch. Most people do that every day, but it's really a treat for me. Usually, I'm out of the door with a smoothie or grabbing some kind of bar while multi-tasking in the house. After that, I decided that I deserve to shower. (Selfish, right?) I forgot all about that two-mile run and that extra ab work. I took a really nice, hot shower. I took my time. I noticed the sun was coming out. Then, I also noticed that it was already time to pick up my boys from school. Once they come home, usually a few more things get done around the house. I throw in more laundry or clean up the kitchen or whatever else it is that I could be doing. Today I decided not to. We hadn't seen each other all day. They had stories to tell me and I had lots of snuggles to give them. I still hadn't sat on the couch. I'm pretty sure that when you slack off, you're supposed to do that. I already succumbed to slacking off today. I need to make sure I do it right.

    I have caught my breath now. I need to feed them, but I think leftovers are in order for tonight. I probably should fold some of that laundry after dinner... Nope! Checked the movie listings instead. Looks like Friday night movie night for us!! I could really get used to this relaxing stuff… Yeah, you and I both know that won't happen!!

Now, seriously…. a donut?!?!?!

42 and 1 to Grow~

I know I still have quite a bit to learn and that we all have varying experiences and different knowledge to share. I am going to share 43 bits of knowledge I have learned through the years I have behind me. I am 42, but I'm a big believer in the "One to grow" thing. So, here is some (possibly useless) knowledge from Kelly, in no particular order.

1. Poop smell does not come off your hands right away no matter how many times you wash them. You are either a liar or practicing witchcraft if you say it does. Change a diaper or wipe your toddler and get some under your fingernails? Good luck! Wash your hands. Wash them three times. An hour later you're eating some chips, you bring your hand up to your mouth to put one inside, and GUARANTEED you smell shit! Don't tell me you don't. Liar.

2. Everything is relative. Some people's big stuff is not the same as others, but it can still hurt or be joyful depending on the person and the circumstances. Never discount someone's pain and never be a joy kill. We are leading different lives. It's all important to someone, even if it's not important to you.

3. Lazy sucks. Don't be lazy. It gets you no where fast and it's annoying to others.

4. Playdoh sucks. It gets in the rug. It gets hair in it. It gets dirt in it. It breaks apart and you find it everywhere for months. If you have kids, you know what I mean. If you don't mind it, then you aren't the one cleaning up after your children. If you like someone at all, do not buy their kid Playdoh for a gift. If you don't like them, then knock yourself out. That'll teach 'em!

5. It's ok to sit still and not do stuff. I am working on this one. I envy people that give themselves a

chance to sit and relax. Don't beat yourself up the way I do when I give myself downtime.

6. EVERYTHING in moderation. Food, booze, exercise, a hobby, people....

7. Don't do something for someone who doesn't know how to do the task themselves unless you show them how they can do it next time. They may still need some help in the future, but you are arming them with a new skill. This is invaluable!

8. Never stop learning. Seek new skills. Seek new hobbies. You will feel badass. I promise.

9. Volunteer. There is nothing like putting your own shit in perspective by working with someone who needs you and teaches you about what is and is not important in life.

10. We all need help sometime. Help when you can. Ask for help and take the help when you need it.

11. Everyone is insecure about something. Remember this when you feel insecure. Think of how you would see yourself from the outside if you were a stranger. Odds are that nobody is focusing on you or your insecurities the way you think they are.

12. Eat what you want, but then burn it off. Nothing in life is free, including calories! Don't go nuts eating crap, then you don't need to go nuts burning it off.

13. On that same note, food is medicine. Good or bad. Value that shit.

14. Olive oil. If you want your kids to eat it (or just want it to be good in general), put olive oil on it. Cook everything with olive oil. Sauté any vegetable you can find in olive oil and add salt and pepper. Suddenly, they will fight over the brussel sprouts! No joke. Use the whole effing bottle if you need to. Oil and salt fix every.single.food. (Well maybe not cake or ice cream.)

15. If you use enough smelly body lotion, you can get away without a shower. But not for more than 2 days. Don't do that. Then you're just gross.

16. If you feel like crap, force yourself to shower. Then dress in something that is cute. Look in the mirror. You will not see someone who looks like shit. This may help you function for the day at least. This is especially true if you're sad.

17. Don't pity anyone. Ever. If someone is in unfortunate circumstances, and you are able to help them, then do it. If you can only offer support or words of encouragement and hope, then do it. Pity doesn't get anyone anywhere.

18. Some people will always look for drama. Life is easier when those are not your people.

19. Bleach wipes. Buy them in bulk. Keep them everywhere.

20. Stay active. Never stop moving, no matter how slow. Move it or lose it is a true story!

21. Say Thank you. Nobody owes you a thing, not even common courtesy, unfortunately.

Thank you goes a long way to reinforce doing the right thing.

22. Say Please. Why not? Again, a little goes a long way. Oh, and if you're in a bad mood or feeling nasty, at least saying please will make you seem a bit sweeter.

23. When a kid asks you to read them a story, you have to say yes. It's a rule, or it should be. Every time a child is read to, they are learning to read. Every time a child is read to, they are relishing the attention. They are relaxing and so are you. And honestly, what does it take to read most kids books? 5 or 10 minutes, tops! Put your phone down. Stop folding

laundry. Make that phone call in 10 minutes instead of now. Read the book.

24. You can't possibly spoil a baby. Hug them. Love them. Kiss them. They need that shit. So do you.

25. NEVER wake a sleeping baby or toddler. NEVER. I don't care if it keeps them up later. Waking them when they are asleep is like asking to see Satan. I would much rather have them lay in bed with me watching Disney Jr. while I sleep, if they are still awake at night, than have my entire afternoon or dinnertime and everything I need to do complete crap because the kid was grouchy.

26. Just say NO to slime! Tell them to leave that shit at school or camp or their friend's houses! Slime is worse than Playdoh! You will never think your saline solution will run out in 2 days until you let your kids make slime. You will buy gallon sized glue! The only time you should see gallon sized glue is in a school or daycare for Pete's sake!! No Slime!

27. Go with your gut. If something doesn't seem right, then it probably isn't.

28. Pick your battles. You really don't need to win them all. Sometimes you'll just be dealing with an asshole and it's better to walk away.

29. If you're an exhausted parent, Wendy's or McDonalds is a top-notch meal for your kids.

Don't beat yourself up over it. Popcorn can count as breakfast if you haven't grocery shopped yet and the kids need to catch the bus. Hey, they're fed, aren't they?

30. Watch the sunset. Often. Watch the sunrise if you're up that early cause that shits cool too.

31. Learn how to drive stick and write in cursive.

32. Keep your friends. Savor them. Be good to them. Someday they might be the only support you have left.

33. Listen to music, loud and often. Sing It! Turn that radio up! Get lost in a great song. It's free therapy!

34. It's perfectly acceptable to laugh at yourself. You're going to do stupid stuff. We all do. Laugh it off and let it go. Trust me, someone, somewhere, is probably laughing at you right now.

35. Be nice to your mail carrier and sanitation engineer. They are there through all weather, making sure we get taken care of, so smile and say "thank you"!

36. Travel. Often. A lot. Travel is by far the BEST way to spend your money (after the necessities of course, since you need to eat as well). I have seen 42 states and 4 countries and I am chomping at the bit to add to that list of places I've been. My children have already seen 28 states. It's not as expensive as one would think. Plan it out or just jump in the car and go! The things that you think will drive you crazy will become some of the best memories you ever make. Like when Brody learned to pee in a bottle in

the Jeep on 95 in New Jersey traffic while Hanna screamed about how it was so gross. Then he did it the rest of the trip so the baby wanted to try too. Well, one time he ended up peeing in Hanna's face in New Orleans traffic. Good times, but I digress. Travel. Just go.

37. Join a team. The support and comradery you will experience is unparalleled.

38. Get to know people. They will surprise you, for better or worse. People that come off as snobby, many times are just shy. People who seem sweet and nice, aren't always trustworthy. Before you create an opinion about a person, learn a little first.

39. Get your butt outside! I love summer and could soak up sun and never get bored. Winter comes and I'm too freaking cold. I am still way happier though when I bundle up and get some fresh air. As humans we need nature. We need sun. We need fresh,

outdoor air! So, throw your long johns on and get some!!

40. Root for the home team. Nobody wants to hang with that annoying person talking crap about every one else's favorite team. Unless you grew up in another state and bring that pride with you when you moved here, don't go against the home team. Don't be that person.

41. Celebrate your birthdays! Do it big! Have a birthday month! Screw the people that think you're annoying! If you're here on earth to live and breathe and get another year, LIVE IT UP!! Growing older is not something everyone gets to do. Too many people die too young. They didn't get to live more years, but you do! Savor each and every one of them! Party like a rock star! You deserve it baby!

42. Life changes in a heartbeat. Sometimes in good ways and sometimes in bad ones. LIVE!!

Don't ponder too long. Have fun!!!!! Do the things you want to do NOW. Be with the people that make your day brighter NOW!!!!! Savor every second and LOVE the shit out of your life!!!!!

I Believe~

I have been a huge fan of Christmas ever since I can remember. When I say huge fan, I mean I am one of those crazy people that you might (most likely) find listening to Christmas music in September. I start picking presents up in the summer and tucking them away. The wheels turn with me thinking about the fun surprises to plan for the kids and for my friends. As far as I'm concerned there are two seasons: Christmas and summer. I hate being cold, but I love the magic.

The holidays are hard for many people and I get that, especially this year. It's my first Christmas without my dad. This makes it really difficult and sometimes quite emotional. My mom died on December 23rd, 17 years ago. I still cry at mass every Christmas Eve. However, my mom is the biggest reason I love Christmas. She loved it too! We had so many traditions that we looked forward to and shared. I get to keep those and share them with my own children. That's a blessing! At

Christmas especially, I get to make those foods that give me the tastes and smells that bring me back to my childhood, to my family. I miss them so much! This is a way to have them again! This joyous season, when people get depressed and think about what they are missing or what they can't do or buy, I am praying that you see the good! Believe in the magic! There are so many really hard life events, but there are also amazing ones! We can focus on the stories of horror and sorrow or we can choose the ones that exhibit kindness and joy! You choose!

We all need something to believe in. Our happiness, our attitudes are always up to us, our reactions, and how we choose to view any given situation. Last year, my 12-year-old told me that some kids in her class don't believe in Santa Claus. She asked me if I believed in Santa.

I explained it like this. We believe in God, even though we don't see him. We can see the good around us. We can see everything that our faith has taught us that God has made. We talk to God daily (at least!) in this house. We believe in Him. St. Nicholas was a real person. He was a bishop and a defender of Jesus Christ. His status of bishop was taken away because of how violently he fought to defend Jesus being the King, the son of God. Later, he was reinstated as a Bishop because of how loved he was by the people. He came from a wealthy family. He found joy in giving and was well known for giving presents to children. This man's legacy very clearly gives us our modern day right to believe in St. Nicholas or, Santa Claus. After my explanation, my daughter agreed with me that she too believes.

So, this holiday season, amongst the lonely, the sad, the angry, dig deep to find the good, the hope, the joy. Help those who may have trouble seeing the magic of the season. Know that there is a reason for the season. People come together. We have heard that many times people come together in a tragedy. The holiday season is not a tragedy, yet we see the Giving Trees, the Toys for Tots drives, the volunteers at so very many places around the globe! We have neighbors bring treats. We gather with friends and family. We give gifts of our time, our heart, our joy. We see others do the same for us, our friends, and our families. In a time of JOY, we all come together!! This is magical!! This is wonderful!! This is what I believe in, do you?

Joan~

Joan was pretty awesome. She always smiled. She was silly. She was quick to take care of all my friends. She was the best cook I have ever known. And, I was blessed to call her Mom. She has been in heaven for 17 years today, but I still miss her like she just left. I hold on tight to the lessons she taught me. Here are some of them.

Where there is an all-you-can-eat buffet, there is happiness.

There should always be chocolate cake.

Weighing in at Weight Watchers and losing a half a pound is worth measuring out the gross deli turkey.

Tab and Sweet n Low always come in handy in your purse.

If you get drunk Saturday night and pass out in the back of the van, you will wake up in the church parking lot Sunday morning because she will NOT miss mass.

You're allowed to be upset about something and get a hug, but then life goes on and you move forward too.

Dogs are people too.

Puzzles are one of the best forms of relaxation, but if you want to put the last piece in, you need to steal it when nobody is looking.

Card games are competitive and winning and rubbing it in is an important life skill.

You do not want to say gonorrhea if you mean diarrhea.

Women are badass and strong, but still deserve a man to spoil them.

Putting up with idiots is best done with a smile on your face.

Some of the best traditions come in edible form.

If you're fighting with your sibling, you're on your own. Figure it out, even if he is beating the snot out of you.

Jean Naté is one of the most comforting smells ever.

Drama is stupid. Tell it like it is and take life in stride.

Cousins are better than gold.

Parents having a night on the town, friends, and a social life besides their kids is ok!

There should always be a junk drawer.

Chicken and Rice and Tollhouse Cookie Squares will make everyone happy.

All food needs pepper.

Swearing is blasphemous (sorry mom).

Teaching is the most important profession there is, next to being a mom.

There's always room for a little something sweet.

A mom won't laugh at you when you break a bone, even when everyone else does.

Do your nails.

Don't finish an entire box of devil dogs before the rest of the groceries are even put away.

Sing, even if you don't sing great.

It's ok to eat an entire bag of Pepperidge Farms cookies.

The more Aquanet, the better.

It's ok to live your life and enjoy it to the fullest after a loss.

Chew your food 26 times before you swallow.

Road trips are awesome when you have the right people.

The door is always open. Someone always needs an ear or a snack. Be there for them.

Christmas is awesome and magical!

Strength~

I was trying to figure out what to title this entry. My dad's anniversary of his death is this week. One year. That's a tough one, especially when it has, without a doubt, been the most difficult year of my life. Now, more than ever, I need to dig deep. I need to pull out all those weapons in my arsenal. I need to remember all of those lessons my dad taught me, about life, survival, and grace. I also need to remember the strength. When I think of my dad and his life, I think of strength over everything. When I think of my uncle, his brother, and of their ancestors, I just keep thinking of the strength. I am honoring my dad and his memory this year by remembering what he taught me about life and living, and about strength.

Always look on the positive side. Always. Hope is sometimes all that you have, but it will still get you through.

Laugh. Make a joke of everything and everyone. Laugh at yourself. Laugh especially when you know you're being really dumb in your thoughts or actions.

Money is definitely not everything. It's not something to obsess over. It's not something to cry about. You go out there and do something you love and make some money. Keeping up with the Jones's is stupid.

You are the only one who can truly make you happy. Make decisions based on that. You get to live your life. Everybody else and their opinions can screw off.

Help someone whenever you can. You might be all that they have.

Play cards. Sit the heck down. Teach the kids how to play rummy, cribbage, and good ole 45!

There is nothing like good music.

Strength~

I was trying to figure out what to title this entry. My dad's anniversary of his death is this week. One year. That's a tough one, especially when it has, without a doubt, been the most difficult year of my life. Now, more than ever, I need to dig deep. I need to pull out all those weapons in my arsenal. I need to remember all of those lessons my dad taught me, about life, survival, and grace. I also need to remember the strength. When I think of my dad and his life, I think of strength over everything. When I think of my uncle, his brother, and of their ancestors, I just keep thinking of the strength. I am honoring my dad and his memory this year by remembering what he taught me about life and living, and about strength.

Always look on the positive side. Always. Hope is sometimes all that you have, but it will still get you through.

Laugh. Make a joke of everything and everyone. Laugh at yourself. Laugh especially when you know you're being really dumb in your thoughts or actions.

Money is definitely not everything. It's not something to obsess over. It's not something to cry about. You go out there and do something you love and make some money. Keeping up with the Jones's is stupid.

You are the only one who can truly make you happy. Make decisions based on that. You get to live your life. Everybody else and their opinions can screw off.

Help someone whenever you can. You might be all that they have.

Play cards. Sit the heck down. Teach the kids how to play rummy, cribbage, and good ole 45!

There is nothing like good music.

There are men who treat women like gold. Find one and take care of them in return.

When you live an honest life and do what you think is right, you don't ever need to worry about your reputation. The people who won't like you or come up with something negative about you are either jealous or just assholes. Neither of those are the people who you want as your friends anyways.

Choose your friends wisely and keep them.

Men won't melt if they do the dishes.

Strength is inherited and I got that gene. It's a strong one. We Portuguese are made of some crazy shit.

After the bad stuff happens, you refocus on the good and make the most out of what you have.

Strong doesn't mean you won't have a bad day. It means that after the bad day, you get back up again and try even harder.

I picture my dad and see strength. I remember growing up wondering how he could be so strong after my brother dying, then years later my other brother dying. I watched him lose my mom and still be my rock. I watched him struggle in business and still make it work and succeed. I watched him struggle to breath and still be strong enough to keep going, every single day. I watched him show my kids how to be strong. I watched him constantly taking care of me even when he needed the help. I watched him die of COPD. I witnessed incredible strength when he couldn't breathe, but just couldn't let go.

I pray for that strength daily, but I also know I already have it. I inherited it from both sides and I am grateful. I am made of some damn good stuff. Thanks, Dad, for being you.

What's Your Excuse? ~

"I'm too tired."

"It's not my thing."

"Not enough hours in the day."

"I need to get in better shape first."

"People will just look at how fat and out of shape I am."

"I have too many other things to worry about."

"I don't like to sweat."

"I don't even know what to wear."

"I don't like to be around a lot of people."

"It's just not my crowd."

"It's pricey to join."

"I have a bad back/knees/other health issue."

I have spent most of my life being active. I was overweight as a kid and hated it. I was always attracted to being in a gym. The people there were healthy and seemed so bright and cheerful. I started running after high school because one of my friends lost weight that way. I HATED running. The first mile I "ran" took me 13 minutes. I know there are people that could have walked it faster, but I was ok with that. I was proud that I got off my ass. I decided to do it again. Then I did it again. Then I went 2 miles. I lost weight that summer, 30 pounds! I started to go further and got faster. I decided to pursue a degree in Exercise Science. It was fascinating to me how something as simple as moving more could help so many aspects of our lives!

Throughout college, I worked in a gym, led fitness classes of all sorts, and personal trained clients. I graduated and ran a few marathons. My social time was usually on the road training with a group or in the gym. I wanted in on whatever was happening. Racquetball, tennis, road races, classes, volleyball on the beach...count me in!! Being active always made me happy.

Flash forward to mom life. I kept running and staying active throughout all of my pregnancies. I ran up until 3 days before I delivered my first and completed a half marathon while pregnant with my first two. I bought the treadmill. Then the weights, the yoga mats, and the dvds. I created a pretty cool gym in the basement. I woke up at 5am to workout before the kids got up and life got crazy. It was the only way to fit it in and I had to make it work to stay sane. I did make that work for years.

Then Bobby died. Then I never got a break. I never got out of the house. Working out still happened, but it wasn't the same. I needed another outlet. I got turned onto POUND ROCKOUT WORKOUT by an awesome friend. I started taking her class and fell in love. I hit and sweat and was social again. I chatted after class and it was therapy. I stole a few hours a week away from my crazy life and it was therapy. I got back into the gym! I became a licensed POUND PRO about 6 months after taking my first class. A few months later I was back in the gym teaching like I had been 20 years prior. Having kids and needing to use the gym daycare (Thank God it was there!) made me mostly in and out of the gym for teaching. It is awesome to be back doing something I love and meeting amazing people. They don't even know how much they change my life when they let me into theirs!

This year with my baby in preschool, it has given me a chance to REALLY get back into the gym. I have started to do other instructors classes, meet even more people, and get into the weight area. I also decided to get my personal training certification again. Helping and inspiring other people is a passion that chases me and makes me the happiest.

I have noticed quite a few things being back in the gym 20 years later. I would like to think that life and experiences have made me smarter and more observant. People at the gym are happy, especially when they have finished their workouts! I have never seen anyone leave saying they regret spending that time at the gym. Everyone smiles. They're friendly. They're supportive! Nobody cares how big or little you are or what you wear. When people come in tired, they leave energized. When people come in stressed, they leave relaxed. When people make time for what makes them healthier, it makes them happier! I have met people that hated the thought of exercise. I have met shy people and insecure people. That all changes when they enter the gym. We are one! We are all on a journey here, for a better life, a healthier one, a life where we have more energy for our families and for all that we choose to accomplish any given day. This is a special place. Come join us! Give it a chance. You have nothing to lose! You could discover an entire new, wonderful world out there that you didn't even know existed! Now, what's YOUR excuse??

4 years Later...~

Dear Bobby,

Friday marks 4 years. I'm choking. It's hard to breathe. Why does it still have to be like this? Every year. May hits. It's raw all over again, like it happened yesterday. The rest of the time, mostly, I am fine. I am hopeful and positive and genuinely enjoying life, looking forward and having fun along the way. But these anniversaries roll around and BOOM! I'm hit, knocked off my feet, confused, in a fog. I know it's normal. I know I am still strong. I know it will pass and the good memories will flow without choking and tears again. Anniversaries, however, suck!

So, another year without you physically here....

I know you're always with us, always listening and always helping. You wouldn't have it any other way.

This year was filled with more changes, as life always holds. The biggest change was the girls' school closing. That was really difficult for them and for me. They ended up both home again for this year until they go back to public school next year.

Joni is a fucking rock star. There is no way else to put it. I am proud of all of our children in different ways, but this kid just blows me away with her maturity and willingness and desire to help me and our family. There is something every single night for someone and I am out driving them around. The nights that she doesn't have an activity, she happily makes us all dinner. She is such a good cook too! She likes things clean and tidy and really does all she can to help me with the others being slobs. She is also hilarious in that very sarcastic, dry way. She gets that sarcasm from me and I am so proud. Her and I go at it like best friends and get the best belly laughs, the way you and I would or the way my family used to be growing up. She is going to high school in a few months!! That blows my mind! I watch old home videos and see her, a little peanut with that high pitched voice and the tiniest features. Now she is a gorgeous young woman. Don't worry, I've applied for my LTC. At least you would like her friends. They are definitely great kids from great families. We are blessed!

Hanna is 12. So, there's that. I love the hell out of her and she can be so helpful and wonderful when she wants to be. But, hormones. Ugh. I am sure I will survive another tween. I hope. I can only imagine the hell you would be in when 3 females get PMS at the same time. She has found a love for tennis and field hockey this year. She doesn't love schoolwork, but is so smart and looking forward to joining some of her old friends for school in the fall. She has gotten very girly. She always kind of has been, I suppose. She loves style, nails, hair, etc. She does a great job when she gets creative. I love that about her.

Brody is still my perfect little man. (Shhh...) He loves football, just like his mama! It's all he wants to do. I try to help him and I am getting quite the arm myself. You would be proud! He has awesome grades and loves his friends. I do not understand his humor, but I laugh. I am pretty sure it is 9-year-old boy poopy fart superhero humor mostly. He seems to crack up with his friends though so I'll take it. He misses you so much. It still breaks my heart. Today 2 different kids at school mentioned something about dads and it made him come home upset. It really isn't fair. I try whenever I can to place positive male role models in his life. I know he needs that. We have a few good friends who Brody looks up to and that makes me happy. There is still a void that I can't fill and that sucks.

Maddox is 5 now. He has more energy than you can imagine and is so athletic! He loves his friends at preschool and will go to kindergarten next year. I wish I could keep him home and homeschool him for a few years at least, as I was able to do with the others, but I wear too many hats. It's hard to accept, really. That one-on-one time I got with the other three, I want it with him too! He is so adorable and mischievous. He is a horrible eater and we are working on it.

He won't even try anything new, acts like we're poisoning him! He is very dramatic about everything. I should have him in a drama club. He did hip hop this past year and his show is coming up. That will be a sight to see, I'm sure!

So, then there's me. The crazy, burnt out, trying to stay head above water, smiling and hoping and praying single mom of four. The lonely is the worst. I miss my sharing partner. I miss talking about the good and fighting about the bad. I miss having a hand around the house. I miss your smile, your green eyes, your arms, and your hugs. I miss so much about you. I know you're always here. I see the signs everywhere. You loved Janet Jackson. Today, while thinking of you and upset, her song "Miss you Much" came on the radio. Thank you for being there. I am trying to get rid of the lonely, find other adults, but it's not as easy as it sounds! I'm sure men think it's a huge score to meet a widow with 4 young children! Ha! I am so busy with them too! I am happy and blessed for good friends that check on us and bring the wine! I am learning with time, that every year that goes by, I don't miss you less. The missing you is deep. I know now that will never change. I will never be able to "move on". I am, instead, still trying to learn how to move forward with you in my heart always. You're a part of me, ever since we met in May of 2000. We became a part of each other. That is something special. That is something difficult for most to understand, but understanding it now, for me, creates a huge step in the right direction.

I do not know what year 5 without you will hold for us. I can only pray that the blessings are plentiful and that your signs from heaven never stop showing themselves and making me smile.

Love you lots. Miss you forever.

Wooden Bats~

I stared out my door into a group of close to 200 people, on my deck, around my yard, singing karaoke, and standing at the keg. It was a sea of red and white, of that famous insignia of the pair of socks, and the "B" that is recognizable by even the non sports fans. The Red Sox jerseys, t-shirts, sweatshirts, and hats: everywhere you looked was the tribute. This wasn't because the Red Sox had just won the world series. This wasn't just a Red Sox themed party. This tribute was to my husband. This tribute was to honor the memory of a man that lived and breathed the sport of baseball and the Boston Red Sox. This is what you do with your husband's friends and your own friends after you have to bury your him because cancer sucks. You take his two favorite things, beer and the Red Sox, and you have one hell of a kegger where everybody wears Red Sox gear. This is where, even your sweet friends from NY that you haven't seen in years drive 4 hours to be here for you and stop on their way to buy Red Sox hats that you know they'll never wear again. This is when one of your husband's friends and his wife who works for team brings bobble heads for everyone to take home, a special bag for each of your children with memorable items from the team, and a legit Jersey that she had made with your last name on the back for everyone to sign with a sharpie so it can forever be a keepsake. This is just what needs to be done when baseball was such a huge part of our lives because of Bobby.

We met in May of 2000. I was all about hockey and football, but always a Boston fan through and through for the Sox and Celtics too. He was 100% Red Sox, although he followed all sports and remembered sports stats like a genius. I told him baseball was boring and that it was a game, not a sport. The guys weren't all exactly in the best shape, after all. This was a common conversation teasing him and him giving it right back. He was cute so I let him talk me into going to Fenway with him. I enjoyed the atmosphere and even got into the games, but still had a hard time watching at home unless we were playing the Yankees or it was the world series. As time went on, I couldn't help but absorb more of that baseball love. For my following birthday, we went to Chicago to Wrigley and I absolutely loved the nostalgia. The history behind the game was what swooned me. That following summer, he and I drove across the country. We made stops at Busch Stadium, Coors Field, and Camden Yards. That first year we were together, I got to see both Sammy Sosa and Mark McGwire play.

We got married on July 24, 2004. This day became famous in the baseball world. We had a morning wedding, afternoon reception, and a whole lot of people back at our house after to watch the Sox vs the Yankees (yes, on my wedding night). This was the game when Jason Varitek clocked A-Rod and both benches cleared for the brawl that followed. Some say this was a night that changed Red Sox history. I know it became important in my house because it was definitely the reason, I had a husband who ALWAYS remembered our anniversary!

When our kids were born, Bobby swore he would be the dad that coached everything, and he did. He couldn't wait for the kids to turn 4 so he could get them into the town rec t-ball, then junior baseball after that. Our first 2 kids being girls, they gravitated more towards cheer, dancing, and gymnastics as they got older. When our 3rd came along and was a boy, well that was a game changer in his mind.

We are pretty lucky to live on Cape Cod for so many reasons, but come summertime, one of the best things the Cape offers is the CCBL. This stands for the Cape Cod Baseball League, the top league for summer ball in the nation. Every summer we can head over to one of the fields any given night and see the top college baseball players from sea to shining sea play America's favorite pastime. It's a wooden bat league and hearing that crack is a pretty cool sound. Watching these guys play is nothing less than thrilling. This is history and tradition and nostalgia. It's hard-working young men lucky enough to get a chance to be here, seeing those scouts at the games, and doing all they can to be taken as soon as they're draft eligible.

Bobby and I used to take the dog down to the field to sit on a blanket and watch these guys play. He would recite the stats and I would always wonder about the psychology behind it all. How did they always seem so cool and collected? How did the pitcher not choke? These guys aren't just college kids though. These young men are the blood, sweat, and tears of the game.

Eventually, we left the dog at home to bring the kids. When our 1st son, Brody was 2, we decided to become a host family for the CCBL. We heard the players stay with local families and my husband thought that sounded like a lot of fun. We got our first player. After that we hosted 3 years in a row, 6 young men altogether. We formed some wonderful, lasting bonds with some great guys and their own families as well. The last year we hosted was the summer before Bobby was diagnosed with cancer and our lives were forever changed. The outpouring of love from my "summer sons" was amazing. Those close enough to pay respects did so in person. Those too far away sent comforting messages and mentioned how special my husband had been to them.

Bobby had always coached t-ball in the spring. The spring he was sick, I stepped in and coached with a sweet friend because otherwise Brody said he didn't want to play. Bobby died in the middle of the season. Brody was 5. His dad was his best friend. He refused to play baseball anymore. That summer, we had to forget about hosting for the college boys. I had 1 guest room and spent the next 4 summers filling it with friends or their older kids who had the summer off and could help me with my kids and give me an extra set of hands around the house. I am blessed that so many people were willing and able to help me when I was left to be a single mom to 4 kids between the ages of 9 and 18 months.

Every spring when baseball season came around, I would ask Brody if he wanted to play. Every year he said no. He said he hated baseball and it was boring. I never needed him to have it be his sport and I never pushed him to play it, but it has been so difficult to see something that was so loved become hated because he associates it with his dad dying. It has broken my heart, really. Baseball has been such a huge part of who we all are for so long.

I have made it a point to keep an eye on where our former college guys are now and, thanks to social media, we have kept in touch fairly well. My kids are older now. They are more independent and don't need the extra hands they did a few years ago. They have begged me every year to get baseball players again. This year, I agreed it was time. We also finally had a player close enough to road trip and visit. My kids are obsessed with our favorite right fielder and it was awesome to see my boys in their glory. It is so important to put positive role models in our kid's lives and I am grateful beyond measure to have that! Brody played some baseball in gym and told me he was really good at it so I asked him if he thought he wanted to play again, but he still said, "no".

June was approaching and so the arrival of our latest college ball players was getting closer. We were hosting 2 young men and the kids and I were all excited, not discussing much else at the dinner table. I noticed Brody seemed a bit distant, sad even, not really like himself. His teacher mentioned it on Friday that week as well. When I picked him up from school that day, I brought it up. He immediately started to cry and I pulled the car over, got out, and opened his door to hug him. He said, "Mom, I really am excited to be having baseball players come stay with us again, but it just makes me really sad too because the last time we hosted, Dad was still alive. So, it makes me really, really miss him so much."

Here is what I said, "Brody, it's kind of like losing my mom. She loved to cook and she gave me that love, one of the best gifts she could have ever given me. When I cook her recipes and smell those smells, I am taken back. It makes me feel closer to her. It makes me sad, but it also gives me a chance to have a piece of her back in my life, even if it's just for a little bit. Daddy loved baseball. He gave us all a love for baseball. It's been missing from our lives for 4 years, even if we haven't known it. By getting back into hosting, we are getting baseball back into our lives in a positive way. It makes us sad because we think of Daddy and miss him, but it also gives us a piece of him, even if it's just for the summer." I reminded him that it's ok to be sad, as I always do, but he said that he liked that idea of having a little bit of Daddy back.

Now that I have my "summer sons", I have realized that Brody really hasn't been the only one needing this piece of Bobby back. I was inside making dinner and listening to my 4 kids and my 2 new big kids playing capture the flag. The true joy of the laughs and screams made my heart soar. Going to games again and screaming when your guy is at the plate or on the mound is an excitement that I almost forgot how much I loved and still do. I am cleaning up more dishes, being eaten out of house and home, and having my washer full of uniforms, but I am also seeing my children have a chance to have more positive role models in their lives, I'm having a blast looking at stats, and I'm in pure heaven screaming my ass off for my guys. You start to care about them quickly and you want to see them do well. As a mom, we want our kids to be happy. As a host mom we want that too. We also want to see these guys succeed, but we know they already have by being picked to play Cape ball in the first place.

I'm not really sure these young men are aware of the positive impact they have on the people around them, especially my children. There is a camp each team puts on weekly in the summer for the kids. My 5-year-old decided to do it a long time ago, the first time I mentioned it. Brody, however, kept saying no. Last week, Brody and I were in the car together. Out of the blue he said, "Hey Mom, I decided I wanna do the baseball camp this summer."

Healing happens differently for every person and with every loss. We will spend the rest of our lives continuing to heal in one way or another as different experiences and stages come and go. For the summers though, we will heal just a little more with every crack of that wooden bat.

For the Love of Food~

Fall and pumpkin bread are synonymous in my house. I don't mean just any pumpkin bread. I mean my mom's pumpkin bread. Every year, by August, my kids are asking when I'm going to make Grandma Joan's famous pumpkin bread again!? I like to wait until it feels like fall is in the air, until leaves start to become orange and red and yellow. Last week, I checked and had all my ingredients in the house. I announced that I would be making it…and the crowd went wild. It was a school night, but everyone needed to stay up to have some. Pumpkin bread is allowed to break the rules.

It makes me think about being a kid. When my mom would bake it, my brother Mike and I would sit outside the oven door on the kitchen floor and just stare at it, waiting. As soon as it came out of the oven, we would start begging her for a piece. She insisted it needed to cool for at least 10 minutes to even cut it and that if we ate it while it was too hot, we would get a belly ache. She was talking to the two kids that could easily finish off an entire box of devil dogs she had just bought before the rest of the groceries had even been put away. Deaf ears, but good try

Ma. If you've known me long enough, then you have probably been lucky enough to know why we obsessed about it back then and why my kids still obsess about it today. Mike and I would eat an entire loaf if she let us.

I know I am similar to most, when I say that food stirs up memories. It takes me into a home movie that's been safely tucked back into my brain. Creating the smells and tastes that my mother created before me is like looking through a photo album. I see the faces and remember the stories. I couldn't love that more! My favorite part of cooking and baking is what I'm giving to my children. It's more than food. It's a connection for them, to me and to where they come from. I grew up in a home where food brought people together and was shared and enjoyed. It's in my blood to continue to celebrate all it gives.

My mom's pumpkin bread and the memory it gives me with my brother is so wonderful to me. It is especially meaningful because the fall also makes me think of Mike more than usual. He passed away on October 10th. Next week will mark 16 years since he was given his angel wings. I was a lucky girl to have a big brother. We fought sometimes, usually over the tv, food, or the front seat in the car, but he had my back. I always knew that he did. He was just a normal, genuine guy. He had quite a few friends. His personality attracted people, especially his sense of humor.

I do have tons of memories with Mike of so many different things, but the ones involving food seem to stand out. I guess when you're both fat kids, that would happen! We also were blessed with a mother who really did know how to cook! I remember her shepherds pie. I make that now for my own family. As a kid, I hated the mashed potatoes and my brother hated the meat. It was the perfect team. We switched and gave each other what we didn't want. We wouldn't dare waste food! We fought over mom's deviled cocktail meatballs. Fresh bread was heaven and still makes my inner fat kid smile. Bringing freshly baked malasadas dripping grease through the paper bag into my house was the equivalent to waving the red flag at the bull run. Good luck getting out alive when Mike and Kelly ran your way! My parents would take us to a place called The Riverside where kids would "pay what you weigh". They may have paid more than other parents, but it sure must have been cheaper than paying for what we would usually order. On that same note, buffets were the best! Mike and I heard that word and became instantly giddy.

    Ice cream has always been a big thing for us. When Mike was probably a tween or so, he entered a hot fudge sundae eating contest. He said he just wanted a free sundae and he certainly enjoyed just that! One of his favorite things to eat was a brownie sundae: fudge brownie, vanilla ice cream, hot fudge, whipped cream, and a cherry. It became well known as his thing amongst his friends.

    Sunday mornings my mom would always get us out of bed by promising to go out to breakfast after church.

I continue this tradition with my children. Sunday morning breakfasts are the best! The week is crazy and hectic and we don't always get a chance to connect, but we can count on Sunday mornings. When we got older and my mom worked, she didn't always want to cook and my dad would be the first to take us out. I recall many dinners at the Ground Round in the mall near my house with my parents and Mike. We all went in so many directions all day, but this gave us the captive audience. I remember times when it was hard to chew and swallow because of laughing so hard. Again, food bringing us together.

Mike could always make me laugh. I know so many others that would say the same. We all have great stories about him and they're always about something hilarious he said or did. I am blessed to still have his friends in my life that can help me keep his memory alive for my children. I am especially grateful for the ones who help me celebrate his life every year with a brownie sundae.

Thanks Mom~

I remember the day clearly. It was eighteen years ago, but still it's all burned into my memories like it was yesterday. I remember my dad needing his pills and all of us being so tired, but just not wanting to leave her side. She knew that too. Moms and their kids, that's special stuff right there. I remember the ICU nurse telling me that I needed to do whatever it was that would make me feel best, since these are moments we never get back. I finally decided that since nobody would leave without me, I would go home so we could all get some sleep. The next day, we woke up and drove straight back to Boston. We walked into the ICU at 11:59am. The nurses grabbed us to come in right away because she was passing. We went and prayed over my mom as she passed away at noon on December 23, 2001. She had battled leukemia for just 3 short months. It was a whirlwind. I remember my aunt telling me her clock was blinking noon when she walked in the bedroom, but only that clock and she hadn't lost power. She knew that was my mom's sign to her that she had passed. They were very close sisters.

The days that followed were so strange. It was surreal. How could my mom be gone? She was 62. I was 25. That just isn't fair. Thank God for friends. They were there, supporting me and my family with whatever we needed. Most of the time I didn't even know what it was I needed.

It's a really hard thing, to lose someone so close to you. It's impossible to reason or to even have a healthy perspective. That takes time. I didn't like that it took time. I wanted to be ok right away. But I wasn't. Not even close. I didn't give up. I never do. I had two great parents that showed me giving up is never an option. It's all how you move forward. I got married without my mom and had kids without my mom. I am so grateful that she is inside of me in so many ways. I am also grateful for the women who stepped up to help me when I had no clue and no direction.

It's funny. I am ok now. I still miss her like hell, but I'm ok. I wonder how it would have been if she were still alive. She always wanted grandchildren. I know that I would not have to leave my kids alone as much. My house would be neater. I would probably be able to cook less too, even though I love it. I wonder if I would be a different mom though. Our experiences shape who we become and change us along the way, whether we like it or not. Perhaps I would not be as protective. Perhaps I would not have started some of the traditions I now have with my children. I wonder how they would be different with her as a grandmother. I wonder if we would butt heads and fight.

I don't wonder if she would be proud. I'm a mom. We know we are always proud of our children as long as they're doing their best. I am definitely doing my best. I am grateful for my mom. I am grateful for her sweet bread, her chicken and rice, and her pumpkin bread. I am grateful for her silliness and her love of "a little something sweet" that I too possess. I am grateful I got her legs and her smile. I am grateful I look at the world as a good place, people as good, that I always want to help, and that the glass is full. I am grateful that I can pass a healthy outlook on life and our place in this world down to my children. I am grateful that, although I miss both of my parents dearly, I know they had a rare love and are together celebrating it now.

I miss that crazy, funny, and sometimes Irish-tempered lady (yup, inherited that too). I am grateful for all the memories and to be able to share them with my own crazy, funny, and, yes, also sometimes Irish-tempered kids.

We Do Messy~

Have you ever walked into one of those houses where everything is neat? Perhaps your own house is neat and clean and tidy. There is no clutter. The floors sparkle. There are no cobwebs on the ceilings in those hard-to-reach corners. The couch looks new. There are no water bottles half empty on the table. The toys are all in bins, maybe even with all the pieces. There are no dishes in the sink, no clothes in the washer starting to smell because they still haven't been put into the dryer. There are no curious and unknown sticky liquids inside the bottom of the refrigerator. Shoes are only on the mat by the door. Coats are hung up in the hallway. There is not even little boy pee on the toilet seat. I have seen these houses. I have had playdates in these houses. I have gone to parties in these houses. My house is not one of them. If your house is neat and clean and tidy, I am truly happy for you. I just have no idea how you do it. Do you have children? Does your spouse/mom/dad/etc. help you? Are your children older and moved out? Can you afford a cleaning service? I dream of my house someday being one of these dust bunny free spaces. I try hard to achieve it, but, for now, we do messy.

I have four kids. I am a single mom. I would like to think that I am rocking this gig just based on the fact that my children are fed and clothed and have Wi-Fi. However, things are messy. The house is messy. We have stuff. No matter how much I seem to throw away, it seems like it just keeps coming out of nowhere. We have busy, messy lives. This leaves me minimal time for cleaning. Speaking of messy lives… We do not do anything seamlessly. There is nothing graceful about our messy life. We lay out everything for school the night before, but inevitably the morning is rushed. We oversleep or someone can't find breakfast or their shoes or both. We do screaming and hurrying and oh-so-messy to get out the door for school and work. I take the back roads to try to make it faster and avoid traffic while we check the clock. Then I drop the high schooler off with just enough time for her to fly to class and not be marked late. We finish doing drop offs and I get my messy 'have a good day' kisses and get back in the very messy car. Yes, the car... I get in other vehicles sometimes and they are so clean. It's like a witch must own it. There is nothing sticky in the door handle. There is no moldy food stuck to the floor in the backseat. There are no empty water bottles that fall out when they open the door. A witch...my only explanation. I drive to work in my messy car and tell myself I really need a trash bag and 5 minutes to clean this up. I work at 3 different gyms. Also, those 4 kids I have, yeah, they go to 3 different schools in 2 different towns. So, I drive and drive and drive (in my messy car). I get home sometimes with time to shower or eat lunch before I need to start to pick everyone up in the afternoon. As I look for lunch, I realize I haven't gotten groceries in a while. I figure out what to eat, but it is a messy process. I shower as fast as I can, thinking that maybe it will give me time to clean something. It rarely does. After school is as messy as it can get. Pick one up at 2:20, next one at 4, then onto the 3rd. They get in the messy car and head to our messy house. I yell about not leaving backpacks right in front of the doorway. I ask them to please not be so messy. It doesn't matter. I walk in and trip over shoes that could have just as easily gone on the shoe mat as they did in the middle of the kitchen. They're hungry and want a snack even though I'm going to start supper. Oh, and I should mention the microwave broke! Try living without a microwave with 4 kiddos. Two words: pioneer days. I listen to their stories about the day. They all talk at once. Its very messy. Then they fight. Again. And again. And again. Sometimes I wish I could just tie them together and hose them down. Would still be messy, just more fun, at least for me. We figure out dinner. I get the boys showered, uniforms laid out, lunch boxes packed. I start to put food away from dinner and clean up when I get the text from my oldest (but not messiest) child. She is on her way back from the away game and needs me to go pick her up. By now I have changed my clothes and shouldn't be allowed anywhere, but Walmart. Out the door I go again! About 45 minutes later I am back home. I tuck the rest of the crew in, stare at the dishes (which I hate!) and walk upstairs. They'll be there tomorrow. They always are!

It's not just the day to day that's messy. Our normal outings or adventures always look chaotic and crazy to outsiders. After all, it is again quite messy, but it's how we do it and it works. Take, for example, when we go to the movies. My only saving grace is being able to get the tickets and seats ahead of time online. This way, when we are late, we don't miss as much or, hopefully, just the previews. There is one large popcorn and small plastic cups. Each person gets their own cup that I fill for them and pass down. Pretty much I spend movies filling cups of popcorn until they slow down. Don't ask me what happened at the beginning of a movie, but I do love that, after I finally decompress, I always see the end! I do love the movies. It is usually the one place where eventually, after everyone gets their popcorn, candy, and drinks, they are all calm and interested and I can sit and relax.

A strong family should always make sure they communicate with each other. We are absolutely a strong family and we definitely communicate. It is almost always messy. There is problem solving (one kid stealing the remote for a turn). There is mediating (she said this, he did that).

There is taking responsibility (I saw HER do it Mommy!). There is decision making (I don't want THAT for dinner). There is yelling to get a point across. Eventually, there is calm, forgiveness, and peace on earth (for 5 minutes).

I would like to think that, at some point, every one of us has had a "messy" life. I wasn't always like this, after all. I'm in the trenches. This is survival. This is how it's getting done for this chapter of MY book of life. It works for us. It may sound all bad, but it's really not. There are pluses to this messy chapter. After all, I would never trade in those wonderfully, sloppy, messy little boy kisses that I get over and over again.

Love~

When I met my husband, I was dating another man at the time. It wasn't anything serious. It was reasonable to date and still have male friends. I think I may have been oblivious, to be honest. I was always quite naive. I was being honest when I told Bobby (my future husband) that he should come over and be my guinea pig, tasting the food that I wanted to cook for the guy I was dating! I was really, really naive... He drove the hour to see me and I made us dinner. It was delicious, he told me. We watched the movie that was both of our favorite. We sat on the couch and he told me how great he was at belly button kisses and I was still oblivious to him possibly liking me. After the movie, I innocently told him he could sleep in my room if he wanted. He followed me upstairs and I pointed to one twin bed telling him it was mine, but that he was welcome to sleep in the other twin bed on the other side of the room. Oh, looking back...I was REALLY NAIVE. He slept over in the other twin bed. The next day we golfed 9 holes. I was having a blast. I never thought twice. I was just having fun. That second night together, we went to see a local band. I remember dancing and having a great time. On the way home, we stopped at the beach. We got out and went onto the sand and I sat down. He sat behind me. That was the first time my heart went in my throat and it dawned on me that it was possible he was not looking at the last 2 days as two new friends just hanging out. When he kissed me, I remember I said, "Please don't do that unless you really mean it." He kissed me again. Two years later, that was the same place where he proposed to me.

Five years ago, after Bobby died, I was left with a whirlwind of emotions and responsibilities.

After that first 8 or 9 months, I decided that I needed to get out of the house and be social.

Raising four kids was consuming me. I didn't want something crazy with a man, just a chance to get a break from my kids and enjoy adult conversations. Being social, for me, is self care. I met a few really great guys, some whom I am happy I can now call my friends. I also met some men with...um...questionable morals. Being naive made me think that because I was honest and kind, everyone else should be too! Like most life lessons, that wasn't an easy one to learn. I have had some fun dating and love meeting new people. I have noticed patterns in people and in myself. I have also learned to never be surprised by a person's behaviors. People always keep life interesting.

When I set out to write about men, women, dating, relationships, etc., I did not want to write from a soap box. I am not a relationship expert in the least! I have learned SO MUCH, but hopefully we all have. I have my opinions for sure, but I also notice they continue to be challenged. So, instead of preaching my own opinion on the matter, I chose to do a little research. I asked just over 50 people the same question. I tried to make sure I had a broad demographic range. The people I polled ranged in age from 20 to 70+, varied in marital status, sexual orientation, and gender. There are also variations on past relationship history and current relationship history. The question I asked stemmed in all honesty from a true desire to learn why some relationships are more successful than others. I asked, "What do YOU believe is the most important quality to have to make a relationship successful and do you believe that you exhibit this quality?"

After asking, getting answers, and having a few really good conversations, I made a spreadsheet. Here is what I found. Among single individuals, whether they have never been married or are divorced and whether they currently have a partner or not, the most common answers were "communication" and "honesty". The age range for these answers didn't seem to matter. Among people who were married, claimed they had overall wonderful relationships, and also especially with people in longer marriages, the answers were more surprising. These people listed compatibility, humor, knowing you are equal partners, teamwork, staying true to who you are and being with someone who appreciates that, and knowing how to let go of the little things.

I have thought about this quite a bit and had conversations with others about these results as well. The people who have made it work for years are much more specific in their answers. I am guessing, perhaps, when their relationships first began that maybe the answers would be different, but I am thinking we single folk should learn from them. They are successful because they are forgiving and flexible. They each have humility when it is warranted. They know who they are as a person. As they have grown into that person, their partner has done the same for themselves. Both appreciate the other and their journey. They have things in common, hobbies, adventures they have shared. They continue to be excited to share and create new memories. They have humor! They are able to laugh at themselves and each other and let go of what really doesn't matter!

Now all of this makes perfect sense to me, but let's go back to our other answers from the single folks. Let's start with communication. What does that mean? Think of your definition. Do you believe that everyone would agree with you? Is your definition general or specific?

Would your way of communicating ensure that a partner would understand your feelings, your wants, and your needs? We are all so different. We have had different role models growing up. Our role models, in general, teach us how to behave in our relationships based on theirs. Now, there are definitely times when this is not true. There are people who have sworn that they will not repeat what they grew up seeing. Some do not. However, that then takes tremendous courage, to change an upbringing. Society also shows us various ways relationships can work or not work. Communication is a very broad term. How you express yourself and how your partner expresses themselves may be so different. This makes understanding each other impossible, unless both partners are willing to put in the work for change. How many of us are stubborn? How many of us just assume that if the other person doesn't "get" us, it's their fault? How many people think they are effectively communicating, but don't realize that their way is simply not understood by the other person? I know I am guilty of this. I admit it. I believe I have learned to communicate much more effectively over the past 5 or so years than I ever have before having to date again. I also know that I have thought I was communicating effectively, yet the other person truly did not "get it". I have been quick to run, when maybe a better response would be a conversation and an effort to try to change how I communicate so my partner could better understand me and my needs. Plenty of "matches" out there just aren't meant to be for one reason or another, and communication might still lead two people to realize they aren't compatible or meant for each other, but it also can't hurt to try. Of course, the only success, I believe, would come from an effort from BOTH partners. Remember, we are not out to lose ourselves, only to try for that teamwork for the betterment of the relationship at stake.

Ok, now let's take that other popular answer among our singles. Honesty. I would guess that the relationships with longevity have been that way because both partners are honest with themselves and one another. I would also guess that they did not list this as most important because it's a given, or should be. Who is raised to lie, after all? Honesty is a quality we are all taught to possess from a very young age. We are usually punished if we lie. As we get older, we realize there is a very yucky feeling (or should be!) inside of us if we lie. Those who know me, know that I am an honest person. I tend to be "too honest" if that's a thing. I cannot be fake to save my life. If you ask me my opinion on your shoes or your make up, or your life choices, I will tell it to you whether you like it or not. We live in a society where not everyone wants the truth. The truth can certainly hurt. That's a fact. The truth also stops a number of hurts from ever occurring! Being honest with someone shows respect, helps you to be trusted, and enhances that tricky thing we call "communication"! People who answered "honesty" as the most important quality for them, in most cases, had been lied to. It hurt them. Perhaps honesty would have hurt them as well, especially if cheating was involved, but, in the long-term, the honesty will always be the better option.

I am not going to lie, hearing answers and having these conversations has opened my eyes to my own past behaviors, as well as the men I have been involved with along the way. I am only responsible for my own behavior. They are responsible for theirs. You are responsible for yours. However, I see where more conversations and less throwing in the towel could be far more effective and less hurtful.

Sometimes I wonder what Bobby would say to all of this. He told me to make sure I found a good one because I am young and still have fun to be had and deserve to have someone by my side. I agree with him. Some people are perfectly content to go about their business alone. I like my alone time too. I'm also raising 4 kids alone and that takes up a lot of my time and energy. Mostly, I am working on being me and staying true to that. I have goals, personal and professional, and I intend to crush them, create new goals, and never stop learning and growing. This makes me whole. Nobody will ever complete me. I'm doing that for myself. The goal is for a partner, an equal. It exists, for us all. I am not quite sure what you will do with this information. I can tell you for certain, don't sell yourself short. Don't settle. Don't be stubborn. Be open and willing to bend a little and let go of what doesn't matter, in the pursuit of what truly does. And, if you happen to be like me, and you've lost your best friend who you were lucky enough to be truly and madly in love with, then stand with me in knowing that lightning does strike twice. It will all happen again. In fact, we may never even see it coming and maybe that's the best way.

Oh, The Places I've Been~

My son's class have been doing state projects this year. He absolutely loves researching the states and listening to my stories from the places I've been. I have told him about how he had been to the place that invented the hamburger, Louie's Lunch in Connecticut, when he was about 2. We also talk about how, at the age of 10, he and his siblings have already been to 28 of the 50 states and how each one holds something different to discover.

I visited his class to volunteer and help with the state projects. I myself, having been to 42 of them, was eager to share some fun stories with the kids about each of the states they had chosen to learn more about. This started me thinking about all of the special memories I have from my travels and how important it is to see new places and meet new people. I discovered my love of a good road trip early on with parents that were always up for taking us on an adventure. I learned through traveling with Up With People in 1996 that the best education comes from experience and that you can never learn more than when you're out of your comfort zone. My cross-country road trips with my husband, husband and kids, and then just me and the kids taught me even more about the importance of sticking together as a family. This rings true during tough situations in your own backyard, as well as when you're in a new place only relying on one another. I still have 8 states to see and so many countries as well. My love for travel and adventure will continue, but so many adventures have already made me who I am today. Here are just a few of the special memories, experiences, and lessons that I have collected from some of the states that I have been fortunate enough to visit.

Colorado: This state is the first one I had ever visited on my own, without my family. It was the beginning of my time as a cast member of Up With People. It was here that I would learn about being homesick. It was here that I would learn that language barriers are nothing to new friends.

Denver's weather taught me to always be ready for anything. Four seasons can absolutely happen in one day there! I also learned that as beautiful as the mountains are, I am an ocean girl.
That salt water is in my soul and it always has been.

West Virginia: My experience here always sticks out in my mind. I was 19 years old and doing community service in an elementary school. My eyes were opened when I saw racism firsthand.
I had grown up with friends that were Caucasian, African American, Asian, Puerto Rican, and Cape Verdean and I never thought twice about it. I was blessed to live in a community that welcomed everyone. I was fortunate to have learned about racism in history books, but not the playground. Then, flash forward, and here I am in 1996 doing community service with people from several different countries and states, speaking many different languages, and having plenty of various skin tones. There is ONE little white girl here in this class. The other kids were all African American and all bullying her, leaving her out, making fun of what she

could or couldn't do. It was one of those moments when confusion sets in and you don't know any other way to react, but to remind ALL of the children that we need to get along and that skin color NEVER matters. I was never on the receiving end of racism and I know I am lucky for that. I know even today that it is hard to not be white in this country. I personally think it's disgusting. There is a song from Up With People, my favorite one they have ever sung. It is called, "What Color is God's Skin"? I know it by heart. "I said it's black, brown, it's yellow, it's red, it is white. Everyone's the same in the good Lord's sight." Please remember that whether you are black, brown, yellow, red, white, or even purple, it is always ok to be kind and never ok not to be.

Missouri: The best thing that ever happened to me in Missouri was meeting my host family in St. Louis. We were housed with host families when we traveled with UWP. This, by far, was my favorite one. Opening your home to someone, especially a complete stranger, is a gesture that shows a big heart. The Kennedys opened their home and made a spot where they have forever stayed in my heart. Keeping in touch with yearly Christmas cards was nice. Then Facebook changed my world for the better by giving me an easier connection. My husband and I made sure to stop and be "hosted" again when we drove cross country in 2001. I was thrilled when I finally got them up to Cape Cod and a day on the beach. When I think of my time spent in St. Louis, I think of the arch I was too scared to ride up in, the riverboat gambling, and these friends that will always be a part of my life.

New Mexico: I learned quite a bit about the Mormon religion in New Mexico. I may not choose this for myself, but I respect the heart and kindness given to me by a very good friend at the time who was Mormon and her family. Again, an eye opener and another reason to not judge based on media or stories we hear, but to be open to learning about people different than yourself.

Nevada: Here I learned that telling me that, "It's not so bad if its 120 degrees in the desert because it's a dry heat" is just bullshit. It's still hot as hell and uncomfortable and sucks. Best off inside a casino for sure.

Kansas: Bobby and I did a trek across Kansas. The sun was out that day, no rain. Yet it almost seemed like hail or something was hitting the windshield at a rapid rate. We kept having to clean the windshield and use the wipers to see. After a while, we stopped at a Subway for lunch. We went inside and ate. When we came outside and saw the front of the Jeep, it was covered in dead pieces of monarch butterflies! It was so gross to see! I had a problem for a few years after that, thinking butterflies were pretty! I will always remember it "raining butterflies" in Kansas.

Georgia: I have two great memories here. In 1996, I was lucky enough to be at the Olympics in Atlanta. Atlanta was cool, but the feeling surrounding an Olympic Games is amazing. I was part of an Up With People cast that performed at a special opening ceremony they had specifically for introducing softball as an Olympic sport for the first time. Not THE opening ceremonies, but still super cool. Years later, my kids and I fell in love with Savannah. The gorgeous city is filled with the coolest ghost stories, eclectic restaurants, beautiful scenery, and, of course, it was the first time I visited a place where I could walk down the street drinking an alcoholic beverage! Oh, and also people are way nicer in the South. It's a fact. Not that we think we are rude up here, but you can see a difference as you drive south or west out of the Northeast.

Louisiana: We wanted to check New Orleans off the bucket list. So, one day, we decided to drive from Mobile, Alabama over to see the city. We had no idea that the traffic easily rivaled
New York City. FOUR HOURS. That's how long the drive took. The bumper-to-bumper traffic was definitely not my style, especially not with 4 kids, including a 3-year-old that needed to pee! My older son had previously helped his brother pee in a bottle before, only to get his hand peed on. So, this time, the younger of my two daughters volunteered to help. She got a cup for

him to pee in and helped him maneuver around his seatbelt to get his little wee wee out. As she was trying to aim it into the bottle, I heard the screaming. "HE JUST PEED ALL OVER MY SHIRT AND MY FACE! IT'S IN MY EYE!!!!" This was definitely NOT funny to her, but holy crap did the rest of us laugh! I'll never forget that ride and I am sure she won't either!

Vermont: Ben and Jerry's and a marathon. This is where I ran my very first marathon. Memorial Day weekend 2002 I ran the Vermont City Marathon in Burlington, VT. I did it with my husband and my awesome cousin. We raised $12,000 for the Leukemia and Lymphoma Society 5 months after my mom had lost her fight with AML. It was a gorgeous course and a very emotional run. It was one of the best things I have ever done and one of the most beautiful races I have ever run. A few years ago, I went back up to VT. I took my kids this time and surprised them with a little road trip. We had a blast! Lake Champlain was breathtaking, although cold to swim in and the Ben and Jerry's tour and free ice cream was definitely a hit for us all!

Maine: I had never really grown up going to Maine, since we always spent the summers on the

Cape or went south. I didn't grow up skiing either. For a few years before my husband died, we would see friends on social media posting their pictures from Point Sebago Resort up in Casco.

It looked like so much fun, a modern day "Dirty Dancing" type vacation. I was far more into travelling and planning new adventures than Bobby, so we never got up there. Then he died in May of 2015. I decided that this was going to be the summer. I called and booked a cabin. I packed up a weeks worth of everything I could think we would need and drove up for our inaugural visit. That was 5 years ago. This summer we will have our 6th trip up there. We all fell in love. I found that I was relieved in a sense that we had never taken the trip when Bobby was alive. It might be strange for someone else to understand, but it gave my children and I a chance to make new memories. We always remember him in the things we do and the places we go.

Up there though, it's different. We don't have to also carry an air of sadness remembering the time we did something there with him. This is also a place where all of my kids can do their own thing and be happy while I actually sit on the beach and read a book! It truly has become the one week a year that I really do relax.

I have far more memories than I have been able to relay in just a blog post. Many more places I have seen and people that I have met. Traveling is the best education I have ever received and given to my children. The lessons and memories are always so unique and irreplaceable. I will conclude with just one more state...

Massachusetts: Well, this is where I have been born and bred. I love seeing new places, but there really is nothing like coming home. This is where my life has always been anchored. Through the losses and the gains, the friends and the family, the loved ones lost and the loved ones born, to our history, our sarcasm (Proud to be a Masshole), our foliage, and the sunsets over the ocean, this is home. As the saying goes, there's no place like it!

10 Positive Things about the Quarantine~

Nothing is ever forever. Good times and bad times will inevitably both change. You lose nothing when you focus on the good. So here are my top 10 good things about the covid-19 quarantine.

1. I don't have to wear a bra if I don't wanna.

2. My clothes never have to match.

3. Day drinking has become perfectly acceptable. (Yeah, I wouldn't have judged you before anyways.)

4. I have saved shitloads of money on gas from not driving my 4 kids every effing place on the globe every single day after school.

5. I have time to clean my house. I know this seems sketchy, but, hey, it's a good thing.

6. I don't know what day it is and I don't care.

7. I have never seen so many hilarious memes while everyone is home on their phones sending them. I love memes!

8. I don't care what time we all go to bed and everyone is less grouchy cause they slept in!

9. Watching My Big Fat Greek Wedding and Sweet Home Alabama over and over again.

10. Online dating has never been so interesting!

Whatever is making you happy right now, concentrate on that. I'm going to finish making dinner and feeding my hungry kids. Then we will play games and watch more movies and snuggle. That is a gift from God, my friends! We are healthy and safe. Embrace the positive, wash your hands, and share the effing toilet paper!

Together~

For a while now, I believe I have heard many people say something along the lines of, "the world has just become out of control these days". I agree in many ways. On a personal level, it has been nearly impossible for me to keep up with everything I am supposed to do and want to do. I have spent much time contemplating how to slow life down. I want to stop and enjoy my children. I want to reconnect with friends. We are always "so busy". There is never a good time. I'll get to it next week. We can make plans to see each other once every few months. All of that is bullshit and not the way I want to live my life. People are important. Friends and family and strangers too, are the most important part of our lives. Human connection. Time to connect with others and to reflect on who we are as well. Time to connect with nature. Time to slow down.

Having a virus that pretty much shuts down life as we know it across the globe can be a blessing in disguise in many ways. Listen, people dying is not a blessing. My own father who had underlying conditions died after developing pneumonia two years ago. I get it. I also have a daughter who is immunocompromised. We are used to washing our hands and many other precautions to keep her safe. So, I get it. I pray for the families who have lost loved ones. But I also pray for the families who have lost their loved ones to cancer, car accidents, the flu, and any other way at all. Losing people sucks. Period.

But, here's the thing. Here is where my faith comes in, my thinking beyond the current situation, the bigger picture. This is where you might want to stop reading if talk of God and faith bothers you or isn't your thing. Because, guys, I believe and I believe BIG TIME in God. My faith is strong and I believe that is a blessing in and of itself!

I have spent months praying to God for life to somehow slow down and give me time to clean and organize things at home and, mostly, to be able to stop and relax

with my kids. I got it. We all got it. We all needed it too! Just because we live under one roof doesn't mean we are connected. We connect through family dinners, conversations, and snuggles. We connect through going through old pictures and telling and retelling stories. We connect through crying about missing dad and laughing about when he had diarrhea on the side of the road. My children connect with my deceased parents through pictures and stories and I smile as I know I am bringing generations together in our own way. The dog reminds us how nice it is when her head is on our laps and just how much she enjoys playing catch. Saying, "Sorry, but I'm too busy.
You'll have to wait" doesn't exist. Attention is given and absorbed and appreciated!

We have the internet. How amazing of a tool is this? We can take time to FaceTime or skype or video chat in whatever way to connect with friends around the globe that we never get to chat with because of working and time differences and schedules! We can still get our time in to exercise and do it with live classes. We can take the time to go for a walk and enjoy things we don't usually notice. We can look up recipes and bake and share goodies. We can use the internet to watch a Broadway play we might not have ever seen. We can decide to learn something new, take a course, learn a language and even do it together with our family.

Guys, the sky is clearer! God said, "You humans are out of control. I will fix this". And He did! Air pollution has dramatically decreased. In places where there was only smog, there are now beautiful, blue skies! People who have had breathing problems will be noticing this difference as time goes on. Everyone will notice this difference! Water is cleaner. Spring is here and we will see it in more gorgeous ways than we could have imagined! The lens on our camera has been wiped clean. Our pictures will be crisp and new!

People are good, so good. They always have been. We are seeing people come together. They are singing to each other from balconies across streets or through internet videos. We are checking on our neighbors like we should have done all along. We are encouraging each other.

We are making each other laugh through some of the best, craziest memes I have ever seen.

Companies are donating food and supplies. Many places are still doing what they can to pay employees. People are realizing how important small businesses are to our communities. Due to having to stop and be at home, many people are now sewing masks for hospitals and getting creative in other ways. I believe that people are learning about themselves and many will change careers or begin new adventures after this time to reflect.

We have amazing people fighting for us and going to work every single day to keep the world running and to make it healthy again. Healthcare workers, truck drivers, postal workers, firefighters, paramedics, police officers, grocery store employees, and the list goes on. Many are working from home as well and this is essential to the world running.

Teachers have scrambled and learned to teach online and change lessons in just a matter of days as schools closed around the globe. I am grateful to them. I know they care about my children. I'm hopeful that they will try and be easy on themselves and on parents. God is giving a new opportunity for our children to learn. God sees a world of people who know books, but not life. Parents working cannot oversee a child in their online courses. That is too much on their plate. Parents home are never lacking for something to do either. Taking this time as a break, for bonding instead of arguing over schoolwork, for learning life skills, and for connecting with families is a gift from God. I am hopeful that teachers and administrators will see and appreciate this as much as we as parents appreciate all they do every single day all year long to help our children.

So, I say God has given us a gift among the tragedy. He has blessed us in disguise. He has changed the world. It needed to happen. We have been killing ourselves and each other.

God has made us stronger and smarter. God always has blessings. They are abundant. We will get through this.

We will do it together. I won't say life will soon be back to "normal".

It won't ever be the same, nor should we want it to be! Let's embrace a new normal. Let's keep checking on our neighbors, let's hug more, let's stop multitasking and, instead, enjoy one thing at a time being in that moment! Let's make sure we shop local businesses. Take time to chat with others. Stop being in a rush. Schedule less so that you can do less and enjoy each thing more! Continue to read more books. Look at your children when they are talking to you. Stop and pay attention. See your old friends more than once or twice a year. FaceTime more. Call more. Just to say hi.

We are all human. We are all doing our best. What is it that we should be doing our best at though? Let us all remember to be kind and enjoy the gifts around us every single day. And let each of us look in our hearts and always remember to keep our human connections and to take care of one another the way God takes care of each of us.

Your Letter~

My husband, Bobby, passed away after a 7-month battle with stomach cancer on May 17th, 2015. Our 4 children were 1 1/2, 5, 8, and 9. Every year I write a letter to him and post it. I write this letter as a way to honor him and his memory, to remind others that there can always be faith, hope, and love in the toughest of situations (and that these WILL lift us up), and because love never dies. I also write these letters to honor the strength, resiliency, and perseverance in my children and in myself. So, here's my letter and here's to Bobby.

5 Years…

Dear Bobby, I miss you. We miss you. That's never going to change. I know that. That's ok. It just shows how blessed we were to have had you in our lives and how much you are still loved. This has been one hell of an effing year. Holy crap! Joni started high school this past fall! I definitely prefer the worries of when they are

younger to the worries of teenagers! She has had a great year though. She has made honor roll every quarter and gotten herself into the health careers program. She currently would like to become a pediatric surgeon of some sort. God bless her! I still hate hospitals! She played volleyball and basketball. She also made the lacrosse team, but the season was cancelled because of the Covid19 pandemic. It is so scary to know she needs more independence and to figure out the safe ways to give it to her. I hold on a little too tight maybe, but these kids are all I got. Someday they'll understand. I am grateful for the friends that she has made this year. They are good kids with good families. I am most grateful that she maintains the connections from her St. Margaret's years. These are families that
I couldn't live without! She is a great kid with a great heart, but it's now mixed in with teenager stuff. She helps when she wants to or when I finally yell about it. She tells me I don't understand anything. She also still wants me to tuck her in and sing to her and she still gives me random hugs. It's all balance, I guess. She is navigating being a high schooler and I am navigating

parenting one. We will both screw up, I'm sure, but it's been done before so I think we will be OK. You would be so excited watching her play sports. She really works so hard and has improved tremendously.

Hanna is 13 now. I am not qualified to raise one teenager, let alone two. Also, forgive me for all the times I curse you for leaving me here by myself with two teenage girls, but teenage girls suck! This year was also the first year for Hanna in a public school. There has been a lot of getting used to things for her and we have had our struggles, but we are getting there. She worked hard as Chip in the school play Beauty and the Beast. Unfortunately, the pandemic cancelled the performance which was just so hard to take after all that anticipation, excitement, and work. She has maintained good grades this year and also played field hockey last fall. She did awesome and I could imagine you screaming and cheering on the sidelines. She is so creative too. I love that about her. She comes up with some of the coolest ideas.

Brody is finishing up 4th grade. He is super nervous to go to a new school next year, a bigger school without his best friend. That part breaks my heart. I will do everything I can to keep them connected though. They have a friendship and bond that I've never seen before and I love it. He misses you every day and most days tells me. He misses someone to shoot on him when he puts on his street hockey goalie pads and rollerblades. He misses someone to pitch to him. He misses so much more than that too. I try. I always do. I'm not the same though and I know it. He is the sweetest and tells me often that he knows I'm trying and that he appreciates it and loves me. He also asks me when I could please get a boyfriend! Ha-ha. I know boys need boys. That makes me love that he does have his best friend even more. Brody is definitely a jack of all trades. He gets straight A's nearly all the time. He is sweet, respectful, and kind. He loves to play sports and reminds me of you in that he has started to memorize every sports fact in history! He loves football, hockey, basketball, and baseball. He is also great at fixing broken stuff and making things work around here and so helpful. Thank

God! He is an amazing cook too. The list of foods he has made keeps growing. He makes his own bagels from scratch and also made a ricotta pie 2 weeks ago. I tell him, and all our kids, how proud I know you are of them. Thank
God they are all great cooks!

Then there is our youngest baby. Maddox started kindergarten this year! He is as unique as they come. Each child is, I know. Maddox is absolutely crazy. His energy for everything is off the charts. He has become more independent this year in so many ways, but he still milks the fact that he is the youngest. He pretends he can't do stuff when he is lazy and wants someone else to do it for him, little stinker. He has made awesome friends at school. We are blessed for these friends and will work to keep these connections. St. Margaret's will be closed now, so Maddox will be at public school too, and without any of his buddies. I hate this. I have every faith in the public schools, I think they are wonderful, and I know he will excel, but they were at a small school for a reason and that's what we all know and love, so this is a hard transition. No matter how upset it makes me, I smile and give them all the reassurances I can and point out the positives. Maddox says he is excited he won't have to wear a uniform because it always gave him a wedgie. He is excited about the playgrounds at the new school. It's all about the recess when you're six. He loves sports too and wants to do everything Brody does. He also loves to build forts and do anything that causes me to freak out. He says he wants to be a firefighter. I know when I finally go grey, he will be the reason. He misses you in a different way than the others. It sucks that he didn't have much time with you at all. I tell him stories and we have pictures everywhere, but he knows it's not fair. He wants a man around too. I swear he would marry me off tomorrow if he could, just to have a man to do "boy" stuff with!

All of the kids miss you. I know that. We all have a void. The girls don't say much, but the boys tell me often. I try to date and meet men, but to be honest, I was spoiled in many ways. I don't compare other men to you, but I know what made us compatible. I know what

I was attracted to in you. Those wants aren't going to change. I was spoiled in that you were a very attractive man and your personality made you even better. I was spoiled because you were funny and sarcastic and could take a joke. I was spoiled because you let me be me and do the quirky stuff I do and you would just shake your head and give me a kiss. I was spoiled and I haven't found that yet again. I will. It's harder now than 20 years ago when we met. Now I have kids that kind of pressure me to find a man dammit! I also have so many other things on my plate too. Every year I grow my fitness career a little more and I'm proud of that. Working while raising 4 kids alone is a challenge, but little by little and day by day I make it work. I have also been working on things around the house and that to do list never ends. I have learned a lot, no doubt. I think about you everyday. Lately, I gave thought to some things I'll never forget. I remember the night we met at The Charlie Horse. You knew my friend and I knew yours. We randomly saw each other the next night at a different place too. Tell me that wasn't fate. I remember being miserable one day on my couch with cramps and you bringing me Swedish fish because I loved Swedish fish. I remember you running out every Sunday night to get Somerset Creamery for us while I put the kids to bed so we could eat it together in peace. I remember you questioning if I really needed to bring my medicine ball when we drove cross country and letting me bring it anyways. I didn't use it once. I remember working out together at Bruce's gym. We pushed each other to be faster, stronger, healthier. Man, that was sexy as hell! I remember when we were addicted to Storage Wars. We experienced so much in our 15 years together! Life is always a journey and we learn as we go. As I have lived these past 5 years without you here on earth with me, I have come to accept so many things. I have also made changes in ways that better our lives and make us happier. I am my worst critic, but when it comes down to it, I know that all I can do is my best. I have made awesome memories with the kids and I will continue to make more. Right now, I can hear them fighting and tearing up the house. There are stages we all go through. I guess this is where I'm at right now. I am a tired mom, not as burnt out as I was a few months ago (thanks to the pandemic for slowing life down!). I know I can take care of shit on my own, even if I don't always want to. I live with the hope that there will always be good things to come. I am proud of us. God, the way I miss you sometimes does still take my breath away.

Love you, Bobby. Xoxo

It's Not Just a Car~

Some readers will completely get this and some will be left wondering if I have lost my mind. You'll know who you are...if you get it, you just get it and you'll know to wave.

I got my first Jeep when I got my license. I grew up in a family of Jeep owners and always knew it was in my blood. It was an '89 black wrangler (back before the 4 doors were a thing). It was gorgeous as far as I was concerned. It was also a piece of crap in the running-efficiently-with-no-issues department. I didn't care about that though. What 16-year-old girl would? Looking back, it was a blessing. I learned quite a bit about how to fix things and at least which parts were which and what they did. That Jeep drove my high school friends around every weekend. Every weekday she barely got my best friend and I to school on time! I remember commuting to the campus of

Bridgewater State to my classes when I was in college. I carpooled with a friend. After class, we would pop the hood and put dry gas in the carburetor to get it to start up. The boys always asked if we needed help, but we would just smile at them as the little flame shot out and we knew we were good to go. Another time, I had an oil leak, but plans to visit a friend in Maine, about 4-5 hours away. My dad was the coolest, buying me a case of oil, and reminding me to keep checking it or I would be screwed and we would fix it when I got home the next week. I am pretty certain my friend thought I was crazy when we left the movies, I checked the oil, and added a quart. I did it every so many miles. That Jeep made me appreciate every vehicle I have had since then that ran with all the parts working!

I drove her for about 3 years. The last time I drove her, I was on my way to work and smoke started to come out of the steering wheel. The next day my dad co-signed a loan for me and I brought home my new 1996 turquoise wrangler. She was a beauty! I called her my Buffett-mobile (after Jimmy, of course). It was, and still is, my favorite color: summer, fun, friends, sun, sand, margaritas.

That girl saw years of memories. She was with me when I met my husband. She must have been attracted to his black wrangler. I know I was! Together we drove my girl down to West Virginia to Camp Jeep three years in a row. The first year, we decided to tent camp. Neither he nor I had ever done it before. It rained all three nights! In the middle of the third night, we packed up and drove to a damn hotel! I have never tent camped since. One year we got my dad and my uncle to drive down with us to Camp Jeep. It was so fun! Bobby, my future husband, and I used to enter the contests to see who could take down and put back up the soft top in the fastest time. Back then they were easy! Loud as heck, but quick to maneuver. He broke a minute and I broke a minute and a half. We won a new soft top and an extra set of new windows one

year. In 2001, that girl drove the two of us across the country. One day, she drove all the way from Denver to Kentucky, but that was Bobby's stubbornness kicking in really. She saw the Hoover Dam, the Grand Canyon, the 4 corners, drove straight across Kansas, almost the entire East Coast... She was the "Limo" that was decorated and drove us from the church to the reception when we got married. She saw the birth of both of my daughters. It broke my heart to sell her when our girls were 1 and 3, but Bobby insisted it wasn't practical and we shouldn't keep it to just put on the road a few months a year (he was sooo wrong!). She was definitely one of those Jeeps where what happens in the
Jeep, stays in the Jeep!

    Our lives took some crazy turns over the years. We had another son, then lost our second son at birth, then had a rainbow baby boy after that. Motherhood took over, homeschooling, and just trying to survive. Summers came and went and I always longed for that damn Jeep! Thank God I know the awesome people that have had it and appreciate it like me and the memories I am certain they too have had with her.

Five years ago, Bobby died. He had bought a nice truck about a year prior to his passing away. That first year, lots of things were thrown at me (as they still are!). About a year after he died, I was turning 40. I had definitely lost who I used to be. I lost her in babies and marriage stress and financial crap and worst of all cancer. It was time to find her again, to get her back. If anything, it was not only a gift I could give myself, but a gift Bobby had made possible for me by way of his truck and being able to sell it. I knew the best thing that I could do was to remind myself of who I have always been. It was time to remind myself of what makes me smile, of the fun life always has to offer if you just look for it. I opened my eyes and looked. I got rid of that truck and bought myself the perfect 40th birthday present, a 2013 4 door sport. She is a cool shade of yellow and reminded me of when my brother owned a yellow Jeep. I named her Little Miss Mango and it's written on her hood, along with an anchor "tattoo" I gave her. After all, like my blog title states, "I refuse to sink". She is covered in fun stickers just like her sisters before her too. See, when you have a Jeep, you need to make it your own. You give it the style and the accessories. Each Jeep is unique because the owner shows their personality. Sometimes those personalities take time to build. Sometimes they aren't very cheap!

I've got four kiddos now. The five of us have made sure she has seen some of the road as well. She has already been packed to the gills each year for our annual trip to Maine and she took the trek down to Hershey one year for a cheer comp. She took us to the Ben and Jerry's factory two years ago and to Lake Champlain. My oldest three now fight over who gets to ride shotgun when the doors are off. They stick their feet out and love the wind. They've learned to keep a sweatshirt on hand and we always have a few blankets in the back. The six-year-old cracks us up by insisting his window be rolled up even when the top is off. They are learning things along the way, like don't eat popcorn because it will blow away and it's no use fighting and asking for Mom's help because she won't hear you over the radio! They know the Jeep code and respect it. They will always wave to you or, my personal favorite, shoot you a peace sign when we drive our Jeep past yours.

There is a peace inside of me when I drive her. There is a freedom when the top is off, when the doors are off. I can't find that same feeling in any other place and I don't want to. It isn't for the high maintenance or anyone that doesn't want their hair in a ponytail or a braid. It isn't for anyone that cares if they get a little wet. It isn't for anyone that cares if they can't hear the person sitting next to them over the wind or the radio. It isn't for someone who needs clean, dry carpets. I have known people who get a Jeep, complain about it, and get rid of it. It's not for them. I know the people who get one when they're younger, then need the "grown up car". Those people are definitely missing the point. I've also met people (especially men) who will say to me, "Oh you are a chick on the Cape and drive a Jeep? Isn't that every chick on the Cape?" There are people who get the Jeep for the "fun car" or for some kind of status or thinking a Jeep is just going to make them cooler for the summer. I'm not judging. But those people usually don't "get it" the way the rest of us do.

Once you get that feeling...once you smile just because your vehicle is open to the elements and it feels amazing, once that gets in your blood and stays, then you "get it". To all my fellow Jeep peeps, my hope is that, if anything, maybe getting lost in that feeling has somehow helped you to find yourself again, too. Wave on my Jeep friends, wave on.

My Big Brother~

Mike passed away 17 years ago today. I think about him so much, all year round. Today got me thinking about some more things I learned by having him as a big brother though. So here are some things that come to mind.

~ It doesn't matter if you yell shotgun, it matters who gets there first.

~ It doesn't matter if you are watching the TV. He will change it and then punch you if you tell

mom.

~ He will always be the one that farted. It will be awful and he will try to make sure you are trapped.

~ His friends will pick on you too.

~ Your friends will all have crushes on his friends, but you'll know better. Looks mean nothing when someone is sitting on you trying to steal your sandwich.

~ Van Halen is one of the best bands ever.

~ Laughter fixes everything. There is laughter out there that will hurt your belly and make you cry in a good way. Find those people. That's your tribe.

~ Just take the teasing and then dole that crap right back.

~ Anal beads really are the BEST stocking stuffer.

~ Snakes suck.

~ A positive attitude is all you should ever throw at life. No matter what.

~ Playing any game is hilarious with the right people.

~ Riding out a hurricane and losing power for 9 days is also the best time with the right people.

~ There are people who can and will eat an entire loaf of pumpkin bread, especially if there is a threat of someone else eating some.

~ A box of devil dogs is really only 2 servings, sometimes 1.

~ When you win, rub it in.

~ Advil is good for a hangover.

~ Don't walk in wet cement.

~ Losing weight is hard, but worth it.

~ Your dates will be threatened and tortured.

~ Don't ever shack up with a member of the opposite sex in my mother's house.

~ Exploring the world is important, but so is coming home.

~ And, most importantly, A bond between a brother and sister can't be broken by death. There will always be signs if you look for them.

Happy Holidays~

It's time for a change, guys. I am not even bringing politics into this either. It doesn't matter if you think left, right, or middle. Change needs to happen and it needs to start IN YOUR HOUSE WITH YOU AND YOUR KIDS. We have been fighting a pandemic across the globe for 8 months. We were improving and now we have a surge. This should not surprise any of us. During the summer, we have more people out and about and less sickness. As fall continues and winter comes, cases of everything will rise as they always do. However, we all know (because yes people science is real) that this is a big one, people are still dying, life is still being altered, etc. There is a saying, "It isn't about what happens to you, it's about how you handle it". Depression is real, mental health issues are real, anxiety is real. They are also part of life. Our children are suffering from these things more than ever and so are we. Professional help is needed and golden in some cases, but not necessary in all of them. There is something missing that we as a society have neglected to teach our children and have neglected to learn for ourselves. It's my favorite word: RESILIENCE.

Learning to be resilient is just like learning anything else, it requires practice and finding the right tools for the job. It requires a commitment over time to change your habits, and even to change how your brain views life and its experiences. ANYONE can benefit from having resiliency. Some people may require more assistance than this, but possessing resiliency can only help.

I am not an expert on mental health or resiliency. I do not claim to be able to "fix" anyone, nor do I ever believe that is my job. God put me here for a reason. I believe in using my experiences and the skills I have acquired throughout my life to help others and to give hope through my own actions.

So, here we are. In a pandemic. Here is some of what I have been hearing.

- "I am so sick of this."

- "It's just not fair."

- "I hate wearing a mask. This is stupid."

- "It's just not fair."

- "I miss seeing all my friends."

- "It's just not fair."

- "But I wanna play football/hockey/lacrosse!"

- "It's just not fair."

- "What about the holidays? Nobody is going to tell me I can't have a party."

- "It's just not fair."

- "My mom is paranoid I guess, but I can't go to that party."

- "It's just not fair."

Let me stop right here. In case nobody has ever told you this, and yes, I am looking you right in

the eye, LIFE IS NOT FAIR TO ANYONE AT DIFFERENT TIMES, SOMETIMES TO

EVERYONE. IT NEVER WILL BE. AS SOON AS YOU SUCK IT UP AND LET THAT

CONCEPT OF "FAIR" GO, YOU WILL BE ON THAT JOURNEY TO RESILIENCE AND INNER HAPPINESS!

We cannot control what happens to us or around us. We cannot control school being in person, remote, or hybrid. We cannot control whether or not sports and sporting events are allowed. We cannot control someone else's behavior if they aren't doing what we consider to be the "right" thing.

What we can control is how we choose to react, view, and move forward each day under whatever circumstances we have been given. I WILL BE THE FIRST TO SAY THIS IS NOT ALWAYS EASY!

You have two options. You either wallow and stay there and over time change your brain chemistry to see life as awful and miserable and to teach your children the same OR you go through the emotions of getting upset, getting it out, and letting it go. Then you move forward with skills that help you to see that life is always changing and we can still enjoy it! In doing so, you teach that joy to your children (and to anyone else watching).

So, the holidays are coming up, a time for gatherings. I myself will miss the enormous open house I have every year. Some worry about money more at the holidays, especially now if you can't work. Some people suffer from seasonal depression and some get lonelier than normal. So, what are we going to do about all of this? What a great holiday season it would be if we bitched

about the stuff we can't do and listened to our kids do the same or hide in their rooms on
their devices…. who's with me? Sounds awesome, right? NOT EVEN A CHANCE!

So, what then? Well, first, let's go back to my favorite word. RESILIENCY. Like I said, I am no expert. Here are just some skills that work for me. I suggest anyone that hasn't done these
things, to start. It can be life changing, no matter how minor you think they are.

- Live with gratitude. Trust me, someone is out there worse off than you right now. Make a list of 10 things every night that make you feel grateful. It doesn't matter how trivial the things on that list seem. Just make it. For example, I ate a hot meal today. I have a bed to sleep in and I have fingers that helped tie my son's shoes! It doesn't matter how big or how small. MAKE THE LIST. EVERY SINGLE NIGHT.

- Wake up and set your tone. Before you grab for your phone or turn on the news or even roll out of bed, make a list (in your head if you want, counting on your fingers) of 10 things you're looking forward to that day. Again, anything! Is the sun out? Look forward to good weather. Is it raining? Look forward to a hot cocoa kind of day. Look forward to getting to snuggle, see, or even talk on the phone with a loved one. Look forward to the unexpected that you tell yourself will happen in a positive way that day!

- Take a deep breath. Relax your shoulders when you exhale. Picture letting go of whatever is weighing you down. Imagine it vanishing into the sky and leaving you alone.

- Practice compassion. Imagine someone who may have wronged you and think of the state they must be in to stoop to that level. Send them good thoughts because nobody should be so miserable.

- Give yourself time to grieve or cry or kick something. Let it out. Then wipe your tears and come up with a plan. Tell yourself why it will be ok. Because I promise you, it will be ok.

- Find someone you trust to vent to about what's bugging you and ask their opinion or perspective of the situation. Make sure to surround yourself with other positive people.

Be aware that some people are joy suckers and some are joy givers. Make the givers your tribe.

- Laugh. Do what I do and go on Pinterest and look up funny memes or jokes. Watch a TV show at the end of the day that you know is funny, even the reruns. I could watch Friends over and over again and still always laugh. There is so much great humor out there and, as we all know, laughter really is the best medicine.

- When you feel down, encourage someone else. When you teach someone something, you reinforce your own learning of the subject. When you encourage someone else and give them kind, positive words, you hear them yourself and reinforce what you know to be true.

- Find a hobby and take the time to develop it. A distraction from the norm gives your brain a break from thinking of the stressors and creates euphoria from the endorphins that doing things we enjoy will give us.

- Read a book with positive vibes, quotes, inspiration, self-help, etc. Then practice what it preaches.

- Use imagery. Imagine you have a force field, a bubble around you. Anything negative that comes your way each day will just bounce right off of you. It cannot even reach you to affect you and your mood.

My list could go on and on, but these can be major helpers on the road to changing your mind and becoming more resilient.

Now let's take this into the holiday season. Let's start by all agreeing that this year the holidays will not be the same, as we have always had them. Now, let's think about the ways in which that might be a good thing.

Do you have trouble enjoying the holiday season because it feels too rushed? Maybe you always have so many people to visit, so many events to attend? Not this year! SAVOR EVERY MOMENT! You have no choice, but to slow down. So do it! Watch movies, bake cookies, craft home made gifts, play games, make an entire darn gingerbread neighborhood! Enjoy doing whatever it is that will bring you and your family joy this year.

Have you always wanted to start a new tradition that can be passed down from you and your children to their children and for years to come? Now is the time to do it! You have time to think of something you've never done before or embellish on something you used to do as a kid.

Do whatever it is that makes you smile.

Can't rush out every evening to a kid's activity or sport? How about using that time at home to read with your children? Even big kids like a good story. Maybe choose a classic or something new, a chapter book to last all season or, with littles, maybe a new book each night that goes along with the holiday you're celebrating. You and your family could also start an advent calendar to open a door each night with a new activity planned. You could start writing a story together and continue it a little each night, giving everyone a chance to join in.

Relatives socially distant or in another town or state? Use a video chat platform and involve everyone. At the end of the season, print the story out, have family members create illustrations, put it all together and keep it to read each year.

Bummed (like me) about not having a big holiday party? How about making it a point each day to reach out in some way to someone you would have had over? Catch up via call, text, or video chat. Missing your cookie swap? Do it anyways! Use video chat while baking and then wrap them up and spend the weekend delivering the goodies to the others involved and picking up your treats in return!

Did you stop sending cards because it was too time consuming? Use this time to send them once again, knowing that getting mail makes everyone feel good and smile!

Do crowded stores always bug you? Turn to small shops for gift cards to help keep them in business. Use time to shop around online for the bigger ticket items your children might be asking for and have it delivered or use the curbside pick up option many stores now offer.

Can't hold your charity event? Do you always give to a charity or do something special? Consider an online event if you are fundraising. If you normally give and can again this year, then there are plenty of ways to do that. Search online for charities and ideas. Use the time you have to help others in whatever socially distant ways possible. Involve friends or family. Make it fun. Make it meaningful. Even something as simple as baking for local workers, essential employees, teachers, etc. makes a welcome gesture and spreads joy that we all can certainly use!

There are lists among lists on Google, Pinterest, etc. of fun ideas for the holidays. Access them!

Keep a journal and suggest the kids do it, too. In it, chronicle how this year you made the best of a situation that you couldn't change. Focus on the new things you did or tried, on the new traditions you have found, on how it felt to savor every moment and to get to spend more time connecting with the people closest to you. As you make positive changes, your children will follow. It isn't an instant gratification thing, this practice of building resiliency. Be patient. I have four kids. If mine whine any squeakier, the palladium window on the front of the house will start to crack. I know how difficult it is to work on yourself. It's even harder to change them. I swear to you though that, over time, as they see your behavior change, they will too. Remember that somewhere in their brain, what they watch you do and hear you say really is sinking in and, eventually, you will notice. Consistency is key. We all have setbacks. Roll with it. Forgive yourself. We can't always be 100% positive and cheery, but we can learn to work through those days and through the tougher times and come out on top.

I am chomping at the bit to get this place cleaned up so we can get to the decorations, baking, crafting, movie watching, and most of all snuggling. I know the kids will complain about something, especially the teenagers. I will smile and just keep the spirit of kindness and joy going throughout the house. I also might pour some wine because…well…teenagers.

Happy Holidays, my friends. Happy RESILIENT Holidays!

Afterword

A few weeks ago, we lost another friend to cancer. She was in her early 30's, vibrant, and full of life. She left behind a young husband to walk through life navigating the widow status, confused, and wondering where to go from here. Death does that to those left behind. It leaves us wondering, why? Why are they gone? Why are we here? What now? It wouldn't be natural if we didn't grieve. Somehow, in some way, we all grieve. We don't only grieve the loss of a loved one. As we travel through life, we also grieve the loss of a job, the finality of a divorce, children growing up and moving on to college, and any number of other difficult situations we may encounter as years pass. This is normal and a part of life. However, what we choose to do with that grief is up to us. Grief never really goes away, but it can be channeled in positive ways. It can be turned around and looked at from different, more productive perspectives. The choice is yours. Something about pitying, hiding, and wallowing just isn't right. Ok, everything about those things isn't right. They don't make you feel good. They keep you stuck. We don't know why we are here and others are not, but WE ARE HERE. We have a responsibility to those gone too soon. We have to be grateful. We need to honor the memories by showing gratitude. We need to wake up every, single day and know that the saying is correct, "you only live one". We get ONE life. After tragedy, it is up to us to move on and to do it with flair and style and fun. I don't make light of struggles. I miss every person that has gone before me. I have had times when I wondered how I would ever even begin to heal. But I did. I always knew that I would and I continue to with each new, wonderful day that passes.

To show that we are grateful to be alive keeps their memories, hopes, and dreams alive. This is what they want for us and what we should want for ourselves! In this one life, we should be celebrating more and celebrating anytime we can. Let's not only celebrate birthdays and holidays and graduations, but also Tuesdays, and that we showered and got out of bed! As you grieve, think about why you might still be here. What do you have to offer this world? Everyone has a talent. Everyone has something to give to someone that will enhance so many people's lives. In my opinion, it is ungrateful to not find inside of yourself what you can give. It is allowing your life to be stagnant. It is not meant for that. We are all meant to be great and to do great things! That doesn't mean we are all going to be famous or solve world hunger. It might mean we are a teacher, a doctor, an amazing friend to those around you, a talented mechanic who is the reason someone's brakes work or their car doesn't break down and they get to the birth of their first grandchild on time. I don't think it matters what you do, but I do think it matters how you do it. It matters that you do it to the best of your ability and that you are proud of what you have to give the world.

Being grateful for being alive also applies to the decisions we make and the roads we take. Don't be afraid to fail. Be more afraid to never know if you would have succeeded! Don't be afraid to try new things, to go to new places, and to meet new people. Be more afraid to wonder, "what if?"

Being grateful we are here, also means that we are kind, that we believe in equality, and that we raise our children up to do the same. We are not here to judge others actions or opinions. We are here to travel our own path based on our own decisions. As we should ignore others who judge us, we should also not waste time on worrying about the path another may take. Sure, we stand up for ourselves if we need to, but if we are creating a better life for ourselves and our children, then the opinions of others really don't matter.

Making grief productive is one of the most difficult things you will ever do. It takes time. It has a process that is different for each and every one of us. It calls us to look deeply inside of ourselves. It forces us to sometimes look at our circle and decide who really wants the best for us and which members of our tribe should stay or go? It forces decisions to be made. It forces us to be uncomfortable, to jump in when we may have preferred wading in the shallow end for a while. It forces our lives to be full of just that, LIFE! We can't stay stagnant and move forward at the same time. I promise you, the choice to become the best version of yourself is exactly what you owe the person in the mirror. It is all worth it. My hope is for you to see this side of life, this way of making grief, anxiety, and all the other natural feelings we have that make us so uncomfortable, finally ok. We all have beauty and talents. We also have real life. Real life can get in the way of our hopes and dreams or our hopes and dreams can become our real life. I'm just here to tell you my version of the story, my own experiences, and what I have worked and will continue to work to do with the grief, the "lemons" that get thrown my way sometimes. Whatever it is that you take from this book, I hope it is positive and makes you smile with hope that there are always better days ahead. Thank you for picking this up and allowing me into your home and, hopefully, your heart.

Made in the USA
Middletown, DE
09 July 2022